The Latest Keto Diet Cookbook for Beginners

1900 Days Delicious, Easy and Quick Low-Carb Homemade Cooking Recipes For Busy People on Keto Diet with 49-Day Meal Plan

Jennie F. Harkless

All Rights Reserved.

The contents of this book may not be reproduced, copied or transmitted without the direct written permission of the author or publisher. Under no circumstances will the publisher or the author be held responsible or liable for any damage, compensation or pecuniary loss arising directly or indirectly from the information contained in this book.

Legal notice. This book is protected by copyright. It is intended for personal use only. You may not modify, distribute, sell, use, quote or paraphrase any part or content of this book without the consent of the author or publisher.

Notice Of Disclaimer.

Please note that the information in this document is intended for educational and entertainment purposes only. Every effort has been made to provide accurate, up-to-date, reliable and complete information. No warranty of any kind is declared or implied. The reader acknowledges that the author does not engage in the provision of legal, financial, medical or professional advice. The content in this book has been obtained from a variety of sources. Please consult a licensed professional before attempting any of the techniques described in this book. By reading this document, the reader agrees that in no event shall the author be liable for any direct or indirect damages, including but not limited to errors, omissions or inaccuracies, resulting from the use of the information in this document.

CONTENTS

MEASUREMENT CONVERSIONS ... 9

Appetizers, Snacks & Side Dishes Recipes ... 11

Basil Keto Crackers ... 11
Devilled Eggs With Sriracha Mayo ... 11
Cheddar Cheese Chips ... 12
Cheesy Lettuce Rolls ... 12
Sautéed Brussels Sprouts ... 12
Sour Cream And Carrot Sticks ... 13
Mascarpone Snapped Amaretti Biscuits ... 13
Coconut Ginger Macaroons ... 14
Cranberry Sauce Meatballs ... 14
Bacon-wrapped Jalapeño Peppers ... 15
Baba Ganoush Eggplant Dip ... 15
Cajun Spiced Pecans(2) ... 16
Pesto Stuffed Mushrooms ... 16
Chocolate Mousse ... 16
Cheesy Green Bean Crisps ... 17
Onion Cheese Muffins ... 17
Keto "cornbread" ... 18
Pecorino-mushroom Balls ... 18
Simple Tender Crisp Cauli-bites ... 19
Choco And Coconut Bars ... 19
Mozzarella & Prosciutto Wraps ... 19
Keto Caprese Salad ... 20
Cocktail Kielbasa With Mustard Sauce ... 20
Sweet And Hot Nuts ... 20
Asian Glazed Meatballs ... 21
Balsamic Zucchini ... 21

Vegan, Vegetable & Meatless Recipes ... 22

Herb Butter With Parsley ... 22
Portobello Mushroom Burgers ... 22
Mushroom & Cauliflower Bake ... 23

Cauliflower Gouda Casserole 23
Roasted Brussels Sprouts With Sunflower Seeds 24
Morning Granola 24
Zucchini Noodles 25
Asparagus And Tarragon Flan 25
Vegetarian Burgers 26
Spicy Tofu With Worcestershire Sauce 26
Tofu Stir Fry With Asparagus 27
Cauliflower Fritters 27
Grated Cauliflower With Seasoned Mayo 28
Vegan Mushroom Pizza 28
Cilantro-lime Guacamole 29
Easy Cauliflower Soup 29
Stuffed Portobello Mushrooms 30
Tomato Stuffed Avocado 30
Strawberry Mug Cake 30
Creamy Cucumber Avocado Soup 31
Greek Styled Veggie-rice 31
Greek-style Zucchini Pasta 32
Classic Tangy Ratatouille 32
Pumpkin Bake 33
Coconut Cauliflower Rice 33

Sauces And Dressing Recipes **34**

Fat-burning Dressing 34
Tzatziki 34
Caesar Dressing 35
Chunky Blue Cheese Dressing 35
Avocado Mayo 35
Vegetarian Fish Sauce 36
Celery-onion Vinaigrette 36

Fish And Seafood Recipes **37**

Steamed Herbed Red Snapper 37
Chipotle Salmon Asparagus 37
Coconut Crab Patties 38
Baked Cod And Tomato Capers Mix 38
Spicy Sea Bass With Hazelnuts 38

Lemon Chili Halibut 39
Shrimp In Curry Sauce 39
Simply Steamed Alaskan Cod 40
Golden Pompano In Microwave 40
Steamed Asparagus And Shrimps 41
Avocado Salad With Shrimp 41
Avocado And Salmon 42
Grilled Shrimp With Chimichurri Sauce 42
Steamed Mustard Salmon 43
Lemon Marinated Salmon With Spices 43
Chili-lime Shrimps 44
Air Fryer Seasoned Salmon Fillets 44
Bang Bang Shrimps 45
Blackened Fish Tacos With Slaw 45

Poultry Recipes 46

Chicken, Broccoli & Cashew Stir-fry 46
Bacon & Cheese Chicken 46
Chicken Goujons With Tomato Sauce 47
Lemon Threaded Chicken Skewers 47
Chili Lime Chicken 48
Parmesan Wings With Yogurt Sauce 48
Chili Turkey Patties With Cucumber Salsa 49
Stir Fried Broccoli 'n Chicken 49
Chicken Country Style 50
Turkey Breast Salad 50
Baked Chicken Pesto 51
Greek Chicken With Capers 51
Thyme Chicken Thighs 52
Chicken Stew With Sun-dried Tomatoes 52
Turkey & Cheese Stuffed Mushrooms 53
Habanero Chicken Wings 53
Baked Chicken With Acorn Squash And Goat's Cheese 54
Chicken With Asparagus & Root Vegetables 54
Slow-cooked Mexican Turkey Soup 55
Turkey Stew With Salsa Verde 55
Chicken In Creamy Mushroom Sauce 56
Lemon & Rosemary Chicken In A Skillet 56

Chicken Breasts With Cheddar & Pepperoni ... 57
Zesty Grilled Chicken ... 57
Chicken In Creamy Tomato Sauce ... 58
Spinach & Ricotta Stuffed Chicken Breasts ... 58
Chicken With Anchovy Tapenade ... 59
Eggplant & Tomato Braised Chicken Thighs ... 59
Yummy Chicken Queso ... 60
Chicken Paella With Chorizo ... 60
One-pot Chicken With Mushrooms And Spinach ... 61
Creamy Stuffed Chicken With Parma Ham ... 61
Lemon Chicken Bake ... 62

Pork, Beef & Lamb Recipes ... 62

Garlic Beef & Egg Frittata ... 62
Chicken Broth Beef Roast ... 63
Beef Cauliflower Curry ... 63
Mushroom Beef Stew ... 64
Beef And Feta Salad ... 64
Beef Skewers With Ranch Dressing ... 65
Beef Zucchini Boats ... 65
Homemade Classic Beef Burgers ... 66
Garlicky Beef Stew ... 66
Creamy Pork Chops ... 67
Beef Stew With Bacon ... 67
Classic Meatloaf ... 68
Pork Osso Bucco ... 68
Pancetta Sausage With Kale ... 69
Sweet Chipotle Grilled Ribs ... 69
Cocoa-crusted Pork Tenderloin ... 70
North African Lamb ... 70
Beef Sausage Casserole ... 71
Italian Shredded Beef ... 71
Spicy Mesquite Ribs ... 72
Grilled Flank Steak With Lime Vinaigrette ... 72
Spanish Frittata ... 73
Beef Meatballs With Onion Sauce ... 73
Rack Of Lamb In Red Bell Pepper Butter Sauce ... 74
Beef Steak Filipino Style ... 74

Russian Beef Gratin 75
Beef Mushroom Meatloaf 75
Beef Cheeseburger Casserole 76
One Pot Tomato Pork Chops Stew 76
Moroccan Beef Stew 77
Meatballs With Ranch-buffalo Sauce 77

Soups, Stew & Salads Recipes 78

Grilled Steak Salad With Pickled Peppers 78
Beef Reuben Soup 78
Chicken Creamy Soup 79
Caesar Salad With Smoked Salmon And Poached Eggs 79
Balsamic Cucumber Salad 80
Slow Cooker Beer Soup With Cheddar & Sausage 80
Cream Of Thyme Tomato Soup 81
Spicy Chicken Bean Soup 81
Citrusy Brussels Sprouts Salad 82
Simplified French Onion Soup 82
Green Minestrone Soup 83
Creamy Cauliflower Soup With Bacon Chips 83
Butternut And Kale Soup 84
Warm Baby Artichoke Salad 84
Coconut, Green Beans, And Shrimp Curry Soup 85
Arugula Prawn Salad With Mayo Dressing 85
Shrimp With Avocado & Cauliflower Salad 86

Desserts And Drinks Recipes 86

Blackcurrant Iced Tea 86
Brownie Fudge Keto Style 87
Blackberry Cheese Vanilla Blocks 87
Mint Chocolate Protein Shake 87
Hazelnut And Coconut Shake 88
Spicy Cheese Crackers 88
Coconut Fat Bombs 88
Coco-loco Creamy Shake 89
Granny Smith Apple Tart 89
Blueberry Tart With Lavender 90
Chocolate Cakes 90

Choco Coffee Milk Shake	91
Vanilla Ice Cream	91
Coconut Macadamia Nut Bombs	91
Coconut Raspberry Bars	92
Creamy Coconut Kiwi Drink	92
Blueberry Ice Pops	92
Berry-choco Goodness Shake	93
Crispy Zucchini Chips	93
Green And Fruity Smoothie	93
Baby Kale And Yogurt Smoothie	94
Choco-chia Pudding	94
Almond Butter Fat Bombs	94
Raspberry Nut Truffles	95
Raspberry-choco Shake	95
Almond Choco Shake	95
Coffee Fat Bombs	96
Raspberry Sorbet	96

49 day meal plan ... 97

RECIPES INDEX ... 104

MEASUREMENT CONVERSIONS

BASIC KITCHEN CONVERSIONS & EQUIVALENTS

DRY MEASUREMENTS CONVERSION CHART

3 TEASPOONS = 1 TABLESPOON = 1/16 CUP
6 TEASPOONS = 2 TABLESPOONS = 1/8 CUP
12 TEASPOONS = 4 TABLESPOONS = 1/4 CUP
24 TEASPOONS = 8 TABLESPOONS = 1/2 CUP
36 TEASPOONS = 12 TABLESPOONS = 3/4 CUP
48 TEASPOONS = 16 TABLESPOONS = 1 CUP

METRIC TO US COOKING CONVER-SIONS

OVEN TEMPERATURES

120 °C = 250 °F
160 °C = 320 °F
180 °C = 350 °F
205 °C = 400 °F
220 °C = 425 °F

LIQUID MEASUREMENTS CONVERSION CHART

8 FLUID OUNCES = 1 CUP = 1/2 PINT = 1/4 QUART
16 FLUID OUNCES = 2 CUPS = 1 PINT = 1/2 QUART
32 FLUID OUNCES = 4 CUPS = 2 PINTS = 1 QUART
1/4 GALLON
128 FLUID OUNCES = 16 CUPS = 8 PINTS = 4 QUARTS = 1 GALLON

BAKING IN GRAMS

1 CUP FLOUR = 140 GRAMS
1 CUP SUGAR = 150 GRAMS
1 CUP POWDERED SUGAR=160 GRAMS
1 CUP HEAVY CREAM = 235 GRAMS

VOLUME

1 MILLILITER=1/5 TEASPOON
5 ML = 1 TEASPOON
15 ML = 1 TABLESPOON
240 ML = 1 CUP OR 8 FLUID OUNCES
1 LITER=34 FL. OUNCES

WEIGHT

1 GRAM = 035 OUNCES
100 GRAMS=3.5 OUNCES
500 GRAMS = 1.1 POUNDS
1 KILOGRAM=35 OUNCES

US TO METRIC COOKING CONVERSIONS

1/5 TSP = 1 ML
1 TSP=5 ML
1 TBSP = 15 ML
1 FL OUNCE = 30 ML
1 CUP=237 ML
1 PINT (2 CUPS) = 473 ML
1 QUART (4 CUPS)=.95 LITER
1GALLON (16 CUPS)=3.8LITERS
1 0Z=28 GRAMS
1 POUND = 454 GRAMS

BUTTER

1 CUP BUTTER=2 STICKS = 8 OUNCES = 230 GRAMS=8 TABLESPOONS

WHAT DOES 1 CUP EQUAL

1 CUP = 8 FLUID OUNCES
1 CUP = 16 TABLESPOONS
1 CUP = 48 TEASPOONS
1 CUP = 1/2 PINT
1 CUP = 1/4 QUART
1 CUP = 1/16 GALLON
1 CUP = 240 ML

BAKING PAN CONVERSIONS

1 CUP ALL-PURPOSE FLOUR=4.5 OZ
1 CUP ROLLED OATS = 3 OZ 1 LARGE EGG = 1.7 OZ
1 CUP BUTTER=8OZ 1 CUP MILK = 8 OZ
1 CUP HEAVY CREAM = 8.4 OZ
1 CUP GRANULATED SUGAR=7.1 OZ
1 CUP PACKED BROWN SUGAR = 7.75 OZ
1 CUP VEGETABLE OIL = 7.7 OZ
1 CUP UNSIFTED POWDERED SUGAR = 4.4 OZ

BAKING PAN CONVERSIONS

9-INCH ROUND CAKE PAN= 12 CUPS
10-INCH TUBE PAN =16 CUPS
11-INCH BUNDT PAN = 12 CUPS
9-INCH SPRINGFORM PAN = 10 CUPS
9 X 5 INCH LOAF PAN=8 CUPS
9-INCH SQUARE PAN=8 CUPS

Appetizers, Snacks & Side Dishes Recipes

Basil Keto Crackers

Servings: 6
Cooking Time: 15 Minutes
Ingredients:
- 1 ¼ cups almond flour
- ½ teaspoon baking powder
- ¼ teaspoon dried basil powder
- A pinch of cayenne pepper powder
- 1 clove of garlic, minced
- What you'll need from the store cupboard:
- Salt and pepper to taste
- 3 tablespoons oil

Directions:
1. Preheat oven to 350oF and lightly grease a cookie sheet with cooking spray.
2. Mix everything in a mixing bowl to create a dough.
3. Transfer the dough on a clean and flat working surface and spread out until 2mm thick. Cut into squares.
4. Place gently in an even layer on the prepped cookie sheet. Cook for 10 minutes.
5. Cook in batches.
6. Serve and enjoy.

Nutrition:
- Info Per Servings 2.9g Carbs, 5.3g Protein, 19.3g Fat, 205 Calories

Devilled Eggs With Sriracha Mayo

Servings: 4
Cooking Time: 15 Minutes
Ingredients:
- 8 large eggs
- 3 cups water
- Ice water bath
- 3 tbsp sriracha sauce
- 4 tbsp mayonnaise
- Salt to taste
- ¼ tsp smoked paprika

Directions:
1. Bring eggs to boil in salted water in a pot over high heat, and then reduce the heat to simmer for 10 minutes. Transfer eggs to an ice water bath, let cool completely and peel the shells.
2. Slice the eggs in half height wise and empty the yolks into a bowl. Smash with a fork and mix in sriracha sauce, mayonnaise, and half of the paprika until smooth.
3. Spoon filling into a piping bag with a round nozzle and fill the egg whites to be slightly above the brim. Garnish with remaining paprika and serve immediately.

Nutrition:
- Info Per Servings 1g Carbs, 4g Protein, 19g Fat, 195 Calories

Cheddar Cheese Chips

Servings: 4
Cooking Time: 8 Minutes
Ingredients:
- 8 oz cheddar cheese or provolone cheese or Edam cheese, in slices
- ½ tsp paprika powder

Directions:
1. Line baking sheet with foil and preheat oven to 400F.
2. Place cheese slices on a baking sheet and sprinkle the paprika powder on top.
3. Pop in the oven and bake for 8 to 10 minutes.
4. Pay an attention when the timer reaches 6 to 7 minutes as a burnt cheese tastes bitter.
5. Serve and enjoy.

Nutrition:
- Info Per Servings 2.0g Carbs, 13.0g Protein, 19.0g Fat, 228 Calories

Cheesy Lettuce Rolls

Servings: 6
Cooking Time: 10 Minutes
Ingredients:
- ½ pound gouda cheese, grated
- ½ pound feta cheese, crumbled
- 1 tsp taco seasoning mix
- 2 tbsp olive oil
- 1 ½ cups guacamole
- 1 cup buttermilk
- A head lettuce

Directions:
1. Mix both types of cheese with taco seasoning mix. Set pan over medium heat and warm olive oil. Spread the shredded cheese mixture all over the pan. Fry for 5 minutes, turning once.
2. Arrange some of the cheese mixture on each lettuce leaf, top with buttermilk and guacamole, then roll up, folding in the ends to secure and serve.

Nutrition:
- Info Per Servings 4.9g Carbs, 19.5g Protein, 30g Fat, 370 Calories

Sautéed Brussels Sprouts

Servings: 4
Cooking Time: 8 Minutes
Ingredients:
- 2 cups Brussels sprouts, halved
- 1 tablespoon balsamic vinegar
- 4 tablespoons olive oil
- Salt and pepper to taste

Directions:
1. Place a saucepan on medium-high fire and heat oil for a minute.
2. Add all ingredients and sauté for 7 minutes.
3. Season with pepper and salt.
4. Serve and enjoy.

Nutrition:
- Info Per Servings 4.6g Carbs, 1.5g Protein, 16.8g Fat, 162 Calories

Sour Cream And Carrot Sticks

Servings: 3
Cooking Time: 0 Minutes
Ingredients:
- 1 sweet onion, peeled and minced
- ½ cup sour cream
- 2 tbsp mayonnaise
- 4 tablespoons olive oil
- 4 stalks celery, cut into 3-inch lengths
- Pepper and salt to taste

Directions:
1. In a bowl, whisk well sour cream and mayonnaise until thoroughly combined.
2. Stir in onion and mix well.
3. Let it sit for an hour in the fridge and serve with celery sticks on the side.

Nutrition:
- Info Per Servings 7g Carbs, 3g Protein, 13g Fat, 143 Calories

Mascarpone Snapped Amaretti Biscuits

Servings: 6
Cooking Time: 25 Minutes
Ingredients:
- 6 egg whites
- 1 egg yolk, beaten
- 1 tsp vanilla bean paste
- 8 oz swerve confectioner's sugar
- A pinch of salt
- ¼ cup ground fragrant almonds
- 1 lemon juice
- 7 tbsp sugar-free amaretto liquor
- ¼ cup mascarpone cheese
- ¼ cup butter, room temperature
- ¾ cup swerve confectioner's sugar, for topping

Directions:
1. Preheat an oven to 300°F and line a baking sheet with parchment paper. Set aside.
2. In a bowl, beat eggs whites, salt, and vanilla paste with the hand mixer while you gradually spoon in 8 oz of swerve confectioner's sugar until a stiff mixture. Add ground almonds and fold in the egg yolk, lemon juice, and amaretto liquor. Spoon the mixture into the piping bag and press out 40 to 50 mounds on the baking sheet.
3. Bake the biscuits for 15 minutes by which time they should be golden brown. Whisk the mascarpone cheese, butter, and swerve confectioner's sugar with the cleaned electric mixer; set aside.
4. When the biscuits are ready, transfer them into a serving bowl and let cool. Spread a scoop of mascarpone cream onto one biscuit and snap with another biscuit. Sift some swerve confectioner's sugar on top of them and serve.

Nutrition:
- Info Per Servings 3g Carbs, 9g Protein, 13g Fat, 165 Calories

Coconut Ginger Macaroons

Servings: 6
Cooking Time: 20 Minutes
Ingredients:
- 2 fingers ginger root, peeled and pureed
- 6 egg whites
- 1 cup finely shredded coconut
- ¼ cup swerve
- A pinch of chili powder
- 1 cup water
- Angel hair chili to garnish

Directions:
1. Preheat the oven to 350°F and line a baking sheet with parchment paper. Set aside.
2. Then, in a heatproof bowl, whisk the ginger, egg whites, shredded coconut, swerve, and chili powder.
3. Bring the water to boil in a pot over medium heat and place the heatproof bowl on the pot. Then, continue whisking the mixture until it is glossy, about 4 minutes. Do not let the bowl touch the water or be too hot so that the eggs don't cook.
4. Spoon the mixture into the piping bag after and pipe out 40 to 50 little mounds on the lined baking sheet. Bake the macaroons in the middle part of the oven for 15 minutes.
5. Once they are ready, transfer them to a wire rack, garnish them with the angel hair chili, and serve.

Nutrition:
- Info Per Servings 0.3g Carbs, 6.8g Protein, 3.5g Fat, 97 Calories

Cranberry Sauce Meatballs

Servings: 2
Cooking Time: 25 Mins
Ingredients:
- 1 pound lean ground beef
- 1 egg
- 2 tablespoons water
- 1/2 cup cauliflower rice
- 3 tablespoons minced onion
- 1 can jellied cranberry sauce, keto-friendly
- 3/4 cup chili sauce

Directions:
1. Preheat oven to 350 degrees F.
2. Mix the ground beef, egg, water, cauliflower rice and minced onions together until well combined. Form into small meatballs and place on a rack over a foil-lined baking sheet.
3. Bake the meatballs for 20 to 25 minutes, turning halfway through.
4. Combine sauce ingredients in a large saucepan over low heat, toss with meatballs and allow to simmer on low for 1 hour.
5. Serve and garnish with parsley if desired.

Nutrition:
- Info Per Servings 8.6g Carbs, 9.8g Protein, 10.2g Fat, 193 Calories

Bacon-wrapped Jalapeño Peppers

Servings: 6
Cooking Time: 30 Minutes

Ingredients:
- 12 jalapeños
- ¼ cup shredded colby cheese
- 6 oz cream cheese, softened
- 6 slices bacon, halved

Directions:
1. Cut the jalapeno peppers in half, and then remove the membrane and seeds. Combine cheeses and stuff into the pepper halves. Wrap each pepper with a bacon strip and secure with toothpicks.
2. Place the filled peppers on a baking sheet lined with a piece of foil. Bake at 350°F for 25 minutes until bacon has browned, and crispy and cheese is golden brown on the top. Remove to a paper towel lined plate to absorb grease, arrange on a serving plate, and serve warm.

Nutrition:
- Info Per Servings 0g Carbs, 14g Protein, 17g Fat, 206 Calories

Baba Ganoush Eggplant Dip

Servings: 4
Cooking Time: 80 Minutes

Ingredients:
- 1 head of garlic, unpeeled
- 1 large eggplant, cut in half lengthwise
- 5 tablespoons olive oil
- Lemon juice to taste
- 2 minced garlic cloves
- What you'll need from the store cupboard:
- Pepper and salt to taste

Directions:
1. With the rack in the middle position, preheat oven to 350°F.
2. Line a baking sheet with parchment paper. Place the eggplant cut side down on the baking sheet.
3. Roast until the flesh is very tender and pulls away easily from the skin, about 1 hour depending on the eggplant's size. Let it cool.
4. Meanwhile, cut the tips off the garlic cloves. Place the cloves in a square of aluminum foil. Fold up the edges of the foil and crimp together to form a tightly sealed packet. Roast alongside the eggplant until tender, about 20 minutes. Let cool.
5. Mash the cloves by pressing with a fork.
6. With a spoon, scoop the flesh from the eggplant and place it in the bowl of a food processor. Add the mashed garlic, oil and lemon juice. Process until smooth. Season with pepper.

Nutrition:
- Info Per Servings 10.2g Carbs, 1.6g Protein, 17.8g Fat, 192 Calories

Cajun Spiced Pecans(2)

Servings: 12
Cooking Time: 10 Minutes
Ingredients:
- 1-pound pecan halves
- ¼ cup melted butter
- 1 packet Cajun seasoning mix
- ¼ teaspoon ground cayenne pepper
- Salt and pepper to taste

Directions:
1. Preheat oven to 400oF.
2. In a small bowl, whisk well-melted butter, Cajun seasoning, cayenne, salt, and pepper.
3. Place pecan halves on a cookie sheet. Drizzle with sauce. Toss well to coat.
4. Pop in the oven and roast for 10 minutes.
5. Let it cool completely, serve, and enjoy.

Nutrition:
- Info Per Servings 5.7g Carbs, 3.5g Protein, 31.1g Fat, 297.1 Calories

Pesto Stuffed Mushrooms

Servings: 6
Cooking Time: 25 Minutes
Ingredients:
- 6 large cremini mushrooms
- 6 bacon slices
- 2 tablespoons basil pesto
- 5 tablespoons low-fat cream cheese softened

Directions:
1. Line a cookie sheet with foil and preheat oven to 375oF.
2. In a small bowl mix well, pesto and cream cheese.
3. Remove stems of mushrooms and discard. Evenly fill mushroom caps with pesto-cream cheese filling.
4. Get one stuffed mushroom and a slice of bacon. Wrap the bacon all over the mushrooms. Repeat process on remaining mushrooms and bacon.
5. Place bacon-wrapped mushrooms on prepared pan and bake for 25 minutes or until bacon is crispy.
6. Let it cool, evenly divide into suggested servings, and enjoy.

Nutrition:
- Info Per Servings 2.0g Carbs, 5.0g Protein, 12.2g Fat, 137.8 Calories

Chocolate Mousse

Servings: 4
Cooking Time: 0 Minutes
Ingredients:
- 1 large, ripe avocado
- 1/4 cup sweetened almond milk
- 1 tbsp coconut oil
- 1/4 cup cocoa or cacao powder
- 1 tsp vanilla extract

Directions:
1. In a food processor, process all ingredients until smooth and creamy.
2. Transfer to a lidded container and chill for at least 4 hours.
3. Serve and enjoy.

Nutrition:
- Info Per Servings 6.9g Carbs, 1.2g Protein, 11.0g Fat, 125 Calories

Cheesy Green Bean Crisps

Servings: 6
Cooking Time: 30 Minutes
Ingredients:
- Cooking spray
- ¼ cup shredded pecorino romano cheese
- ¼ cup pork rind crumbs
- 1 tsp garlic powder
- Salt and black pepper to taste
- 2 eggs
- 1 lb green beans, thread removed

Directions:
1. Preheat oven to 425°F and line two baking sheets with foil. Grease with cooking spray and set aside.
2. Mix the pecorino, pork rinds, garlic powder, salt, and black pepper in a bowl. Beat the eggs in another bowl. Coat green beans in eggs, then cheese mixture and arrange evenly on the baking sheets.
3. Grease lightly with cooking spray and bake for 15 minutes to be crispy. Transfer to a wire rack to cool before serving. Serve with sugar-free tomato dip.

Nutrition:
- Info Per Servings 3g Carbs, 5g Protein, 19g Fat, 210 Calories

Onion Cheese Muffins

Servings: 6
Cooking Time: 20 Minutes
Ingredients:
- ¼ cup Colby jack cheese, shredded
- ¼ cup shallots, minced
- 1 cup almond flour
- 1 egg
- 3 tbsp sour cream
- ½ tsp salt
- 3 tbsp melted butter or oil

Directions:
1. Line 6 muffin tins with 6 muffin liners. Set aside and preheat oven to 3500F.
2. In a bowl, stir the dry and wet ingredients alternately. Mix well using a spatula until the consistency of the mixture becomes even.
3. Scoop a spoonful of the batter to the prepared muffin tins.
4. Bake for 20 minutes in the oven until golden brown.
5. Serve and enjoy.

Nutrition:
- Info Per Servings 4.6g Carbs, 6.3g Protein, 17.4g Fat, 193 Calories

Keto "cornbread"

Servings: 8
Cooking Time: 30 Minutes
Ingredients:
- 1 ¼ cups coconut milk
- 4 eggs, beaten
- 4 tbsp baking powder
- ½ cup almond meal
- 3 tablespoons olive oil

Directions:
1. Prepare 8 x 8-inch baking dish or a black iron skillet then add shortening.
2. Put the baking dish or skillet inside the oven on 425oF and leave there for 10 minutes.
3. In a bowl, add coconut milk and eggs then mix well. Stir in the rest of the ingredients.
4. Once all ingredients are mixed, pour the mixture into the heated skillet.
5. Then cook for 15 to 20 minutes in the oven until golden brown.

Nutrition:
- Info Per Servings 2.6g Carbs, 5.4g Protein, 18.9g Fat, 196 Calories

Pecorino-mushroom Balls

Servings: 4
Cooking Time: 20 Minutes
Ingredients:
- 2 tbsp butter, softened
- 2 garlic cloves, minced
- 2 cups portobello mushrooms, chopped
- 4 tbsp blanched almond flour
- 4 tbsp ground flax seeds
- 4 tbsp hemp seeds
- 4 tbsp sunflower seeds
- 1 tbsp cajun seasonings
- 1 tsp mustard
- 2 eggs, whisked
- ½ cup pecorino cheese

Directions:
1. Set a pan over medium-high heat and warm 1 tablespoon of butter. Add in mushrooms and garlic and sauté until there is no more water in mushrooms.
2. Place in pecorino cheese, almond flour, hemp seeds, mustard, eggs, sunflower seeds, flax seeds, and Cajun seasonings. Create 4 burgers from the mixture.
3. In a pan, warm the remaining butter; fry the burgers for 7 minutes. Flip them over with a wide spatula and cook for 6 more minutes. Serve while warm.

Nutrition:
- Info Per Servings 7.7g Carbs, 16.8g Protein, 30g Fat, 370 Calories

Simple Tender Crisp Cauli-bites

Servings: 3
Cooking Time: 10 Minutes
Ingredients:
- 2 cups cauliflower florets
- 2 clove garlic minced
- 4 tablespoons olive oil
- ¼ tsp salt
- ½ tsp pepper

Directions:
1. In a small bowl, mix well olive oil salt, pepper, and garlic.
2. Place cauliflower florets on a baking pan. Drizzle with seasoned oil and toss well to coat.
3. Evenly spread in a single layer and place a pan on the top rack of the oven.
4. Broil on low for 5 minutes. Turnover florets and return to the oven.
5. Continue cooking for another 5 minutes.
6. Serve and enjoy.

Nutrition:
- Info Per Servings 4.9g Carbs, 1.7g Protein, 18g Fat, 183 Calories

Choco And Coconut Bars

Servings: 9
Cooking Time: 30 Minutes
Ingredients:
- 1 tbsp Stevia
- ¾ cup shredded coconut, unsweetened
- ½ cup ground nuts (almonds, pecans, or walnuts)
- ¼ cup unsweetened cocoa powder
- 4 tbsp coconut oil

Directions:
1. In a medium bowl, mix shredded coconut, nuts, and cocoa powder.
2. Add Stevia and coconut oil.
3. Mix batter thoroughly.
4. In a 9x9 square inch pan or dish, press the batter and for a 30-minutes place in the freezer.
5. Evenly divide into suggested servings and enjoy.

Nutrition:
- Info Per Servings 2.7g Carbs, 1.3g Protein, 9.3g Fat, 99.7 Calories

Mozzarella & Prosciutto Wraps

Servings: 6
Cooking Time: 15 Minutes
Ingredients:
- 6 thin prosciutto slices
- 18 basil leaves
- 18 mozzarella ciliegine

Directions:
1. Cut the prosciutto slices into three strips. Place basil leaves at the end of each strip. Top with mozzarella. Wrap the mozzarella in prosciutto. Secure with toothpicks.

Nutrition:
- Info Per Servings 0.1g Carbs, 13g Protein, 12g Fat, 163 Calories

Keto Caprese Salad

Servings: 2
Cooking Time: 0 Minutes
Ingredients:
- 2 roma tomatoes, sliced thinly
- 8 large fresh basil leaves
- 2 oz fresh mozzarella part-skim, sliced into ½-inch cubes
- 2 tsp balsamic vinegar
- 4 tsp extra virgin olive oil
- Pepper to taste

Directions:
1. Place tomatoes on a plate.
2. Season with pepper. Sprinkle with basil and mozzarella,
3. Drizzle balsamic vinegar and olive oil before serving.

Nutrition:
- Info Per Servings 4g Carbs, 7g Protein, 9g Fat, 130 Calories

Cocktail Kielbasa With Mustard Sauce

Servings: 8
Cooking Time: 6 Hours
Ingredients:
- 2 pounds kielbasa (Polish sausage)
- 1 jar prepared mustard
- 1 bay leaf
- Pepper to taste

Directions:
1. Slice kielbasa into bite-sized pieces.
2. Place all ingredients in the slow cooker.
3. Give a good stir to combine everything.
4. Close the lid and cook on low for 6 hours.
5. Remove the bay leaf.
6. Serve on toothpicks.

Nutrition:
- Info Per Servings 4g Carbs, 14g Protein, 20g Fat, 256 Calories

Sweet And Hot Nuts

Servings: 12
Cooking Time: 4 Hours
Ingredients:
- ½ pound assorted nuts, raw
- 1/3 cup butter, melted
- 1 teaspoon cayenne pepper or to taste
- 1 tablespoon MCT oil or coconut oil
- 1 packet stevia powder
- ¼ tsp salt

Directions:
1. Place all ingredients in the crockpot.
2. Give it a good stir to combine everything.
3. Close the lid and cook on low for 4 hours.

Nutrition:
- Info Per Servings 2.9g Carbs, 7.0g Protein, 21.6g Fat, 271 Calories

Asian Glazed Meatballs

Servings: 4
Cooking Time: 35 Minutes

Ingredients:
- 1-pound frozen meatballs, thawed to room temperature
- ½ cup hoisin sauce
- 1 tablespoon apricot jam
- 2 tablespoons soy sauce
- ½ teaspoon sesame oil
- 5 tbsp MCT oil or coconut oil
- 2 tbsp water

Directions:
1. Place a heavy-bottomed pot on medium-high fire and heat coconut oil.
2. Sauté meatballs until lightly browned, around 10 minutes.
3. Stir in remaining ingredients and mix well.
4. Cover and cook for 25 minutes on low fire, mixing now and then.
5. Serve and enjoy.

Nutrition:
- Info Per Servings 6.5g Carbs, 16.3g Protein, 51.6g Fat, 536 Calories

Balsamic Zucchini

Servings: 4
Cooking Time: 20 Minutes

Ingredients:
- 3 medium zucchinis, cut into thin slices
- 1/2 cup chopped sweet onion
- 1/2 teaspoon dried rosemary, crushed
- 2 tablespoons balsamic vinegar
- 1/3 cup crumbled feta cheese
- 1/2 teaspoon salt
- 1/4 teaspoon pepper
- 4 tablespoon olive oil

Directions:
1. In a large skillet, heat oil over medium-high heat; sauté zucchini and onion until crisp-tender, 6-8 minutes. Stir in seasonings. Add vinegar; cook and stir 2 minutes. Top with cheese.

Nutrition:
- Info Per Servings 5g Carbs, 4g Protein, 16g Fat, 175 Calories

Vegan, Vegetable & Meatless Recipes

Herb Butter With Parsley

Servings: 1
Cooking Time: 0 Minutes
Ingredients:
- 5 oz. butter, at room temperature
- 1 garlic clove, pressed
- ½ tbsp garlic powder
- 4 tbsp fresh parsley, finely chopped
- 1 tsp lemon juice
- ½ tsp salt

Directions:
1. In a bowl, stir all ingredients until completely combined. Set aside for 15 minutes or refrigerate it before serving.

Nutrition:
- Info Per Servings 1g Carbs, 1g Protein, 28g Fat, 258 Calories

Portobello Mushroom Burgers

Servings: 4
Cooking Time: 15 Minutes
Ingredients:
- 4 low carb buns
- 4 portobello mushroom caps
- 1 clove garlic, minced
- ½ tsp salt
- 2 tbsp olive oil
- ½ cup sliced roasted red peppers
- 2 medium tomatoes, chopped
- ¼ cup crumbled feta cheese
- 1 tbsp red wine vinegar
- 2 tbsp pitted kalamata olives, chopped
- ½ tsp dried oregano
- 2 cups baby salad greens

Directions:
1. Heat the grill pan over medium-high heat and while it heats, crush the garlic with salt in a bowl using the back of a spoon. Stir in 1 tablespoon of oil and brush the mushrooms and each inner side of the buns with the mixture.
2. Place the mushrooms in the heated pan and grill them on both sides for 8 minutes until tender.
3. Also, toast the buns in the pan until they are crisp, about 2 minutes. Set aside.
4. In a bowl, mix the red peppers, tomatoes, olives, feta cheese, vinegar, oregano, baby salad greens, and remaining oil; toss them. Assemble the burger: in a slice of bun, add a mushroom cap, a scoop of vegetables, and another slice of bread. Serve with cheese dip.

Nutrition:
- Info Per Servings 3g Carbs, 16g Protein, 8g Fat, 190 Calories

Mushroom & Cauliflower Bake

Servings: 4
Cooking Time: 30 Minutes
Ingredients:
- Cooking spray
- 1 head cauliflower, cut into florets
- 8 ounces mushrooms, halved
- 2 garlic cloves, smashed
- 2 tomatoes, pureed
- ¼ cup coconut oil, melted
- 1 tsp chili paprika paste
- ¼ tsp marjoram
- ½ tsp curry powder
- Salt and black pepper, to taste

Directions:
1. Set oven to 390°F. Apply a cooking spray to a baking dish. Lay mushrooms and cauliflower in the baking dish. Around the vegetables, scatter smashed garlic. Place in the pureed tomatoes. Sprinkle over melted coconut oil and place in chili paprika paste, curry, black pepper, salt, and marjoram. Roast for 25 minutes, turning once. Place in a serving plate and serve with green salad.

Nutrition:
- Info Per Servings 11.6g Carbs, 5g Protein, 6.7g Fat, 113 Calories

Cauliflower Gouda Casserole

Servings: 4
Cooking Time: 21 Minutes
Ingredients:
- 2 heads cauliflower, cut into florets
- ⅓ cup butter, cubed
- 2 tbsp melted butter
- 1 white onion, chopped
- Pink salt and black pepper to taste
- ¼ almond milk
- ½ cup almond flour
- 1 ½ cup grated gouda cheese
- Water for sprinkling

Directions:
1. Preheat oven to 350°F and put the cauli florets in a large microwave-safe bowl. Sprinkle with water, and steam in the microwave for 4 to 5 minutes.
2. Melt the ⅓ cup of butter in a saucepan over medium heat and sauté the onion for 3 minutes. Add the cauliflower, season with salt and black pepper and mix in almond milk. Simmer for 3 minutes.
3. Mix the remaining melted butter with almond flour. Stir into the cauliflower as well as half of the cheese. Sprinkle the top with the remaining cheese and bake for 10 minutes until the cheese has melted and golden brown on the top. Plate the bake and serve with arugula salad.

Nutrition:
- Info Per Servings 4g Carbs, 12g Protein, 15g Fat, 215 Calories

Roasted Brussels Sprouts With Sunflower Seeds

Servings: 6
Cooking Time: 45 Minutes
Ingredients:
- Nonstick cooking spray
- 3 pounds brussels sprouts, halved
- ¼ cup olive oil
- Salt and ground black pepper, to taste
- 1 tsp sunflower seeds
- 2 tbsp fresh chives, chopped

Directions:
1. Set oven to 390°F. Apply a nonstick cooking spray to a rimmed baking sheet. Arrange sprout halves on the baking sheet. Shake in black pepper, salt, sunflower seeds, and olive oil.
2. Roast for 40 minutes, until the cabbage becomes soft. Apply a garnish of fresh chopped chives.

Nutrition:
- Info Per Servings 8g Carbs, 2.1g Protein, 17g Fat, 186 Calories

Morning Granola

Servings: 8
Cooking Time: 1 Hour
Ingredients:
- 1 tbsp coconut oil
- ⅓ cup almond flakes
- ½ cups almond milk
- 2 tbsp sugar
- 1/8 tsp salt
- 1 tsp lime zest
- 1/8 tsp nutmeg, grated
- ½ tsp ground cinnamon
- ½ cup pecans, chopped
- ½ cup almonds, slivered
- 2 tbsp pepitas
- 3 tbsp sunflower seeds
- ¼ cup flax seed

Directions:
1. Set a deep pan over medium-high heat and warm the coconut oil. Add almond flakes and toast for 1 to 2 minutes. Stir in the remaining ingredients. Set oven to 300°F. Lay the mixture in an even layer onto a baking sheet lined with a parchment paper. Bake for 1 hour, making sure that you shake gently in intervals of 15 minutes. Serve alongside additional almond milk.

Nutrition:
- Info Per Servings 9.2g Carbs, 5.1g Protein, 24.3g Fat, 262 Calories

Zucchini Noodles

Servings: 6
Cooking Time: 15 Mins
Ingredients:
- 2 cloves garlic, minced
- 2 medium zucchini, cut into noodles with a spiralizer
- 12 zucchini blossoms, pistils removed; cut into strips
- 6 fresh basil leaves, cut into strips, or to taste
- 4 tablespoons olive oil
- Salt to taste

Directions:
1. In a large skillet over low heat, cook garlic in olive oil for 10 minutes until slightly browned. Add in zucchini and zucchini blossoms, stir well.
2. Toss in green beans and season with salt to taste; sprinkle with basil and serve.

Nutrition:
- Info Per Servings 13.5g Carbs, 5.7g Protein, 28.1g Fat, 348 Calories

Asparagus And Tarragon Flan

Servings: 4
Cooking Time: 65 Minutes
Ingredients:
- 16 asparagus, stems trimmed
- 1 cup water
- ½ cup whipping cream
- 1 cup almond milk
- 2 eggs + 2 egg yolks, beaten in a bowl
- 2 tbsp chopped tarragon, fresh
- Salt and black pepper to taste
- A small pinch of nutmeg
- 2 tbsp grated Parmesan cheese
- 3 cups water
- 2 tbsp butter, melted
- 1 tbsp butter, softened

Directions:
1. Pour the water and some salt in a pot, add the asparagus, and bring them to boil over medium heat on a stovetop for 6 minutes. Drain the asparagus; cut their tips and reserve for garnishing. Chop the remaining asparagus into small pieces.
2. In a blender, add the chopped asparagus, whipping cream, almond milk, tarragon, ½ teaspoon of salt, nutmeg, pepper, and Parmesan cheese. Process the ingredients on high speed until smooth. Pour the mixture through a sieve into a bowl and whisk the eggs into it.
3. Preheat the oven to 350°F. Grease the ramekins with softened butter and share the asparagus mixture among the ramekins. Pour the melted butter over each mixture and top with 2-3 asparagus tips. Pour the remaining water into a baking dish, place in the ramekins, and insert in the oven.
4. Bake for 45 minutes until their middle parts are no longer watery. Remove the ramekins and let cool. Garnish the flan with the asparagus tips and serve with chilled white wine.

Nutrition:
- Info Per Servings 2.5g Carbs, 12.5g Protein, 11.6g Fat, 264 Calories

Vegetarian Burgers

Servings: 2
Cooking Time: 20 Minutes
Ingredients:
- 1 garlic cloves, minced
- 2 portobello mushrooms, sliced
- 1 tbsp coconut oil, melted
- 1 tbsp chopped basil
- 1 tbsp oregano
- 2 eggs, fried
- 2 low carb buns
- 2 tbsp mayonnaise
- 2 lettuce leaves

Directions:
1. Combine the melted coconut oil, garlic, herbs, and salt, in a bowl. Place the mushrooms in the bowl and coat well. Preheat the grill to medium heat. Grill the mushrooms for 2 minutes per side.
2. Cut the low carb buns in half. Add the lettuce leaves, grilled mushrooms, eggs, and mayonnaise. Top with the other bun half.

Nutrition:
- Info Per Servings 8.5g Carbs, 23g Protein, 55g Fat, 637 Calories

Spicy Tofu With Worcestershire Sauce

Servings: 4
Cooking Time: 25 Minutes
Ingredients:
- 2 tbsp olive oil
- 14 ounces block tofu, pressed and cubed
- 1 celery stalk, chopped
- 1 bunch scallions, chopped
- 1 tsp cayenne pepper
- 1 tsp garlic powder
- 2 tbsp Worcestershire sauce
- Salt and black pepper, to taste
- 1 pound green cabbage, shredded
- ½ tsp turmeric powder
- ¼ tsp dried basil

Directions:
1. Set a large skillet over medium-high heat and warm 1 tablespoon of olive oil. Stir in tofu cubes and cook for 8 minutes. Place in scallions and celery; cook for 5 minutes until soft
2. Stir in cayenne, Worcestershire sauce, pepper, salt, and garlic; cook for 3 more minutes; set aside.
3. In the same pan, warm the remaining 1 tablespoon of oil. Add in shredded cabbage and the remaining seasonings and cook for 4 minutes. Mix in tofu mixture and serve while warm.

Nutrition:
- Info Per Servings 8.3g Carbs, 8.1g Protein, 10.3g Fat, 182 Calories

Tofu Stir Fry With Asparagus

Servings: 4
Cooking Time: 30 Minutes
Ingredients:
- 1 pound asparagus, cut off stems
- 2 tbsp olive oil
- 2 blocks tofu, pressed and cubed
- 2 garlic cloves, minced
- 1 tsp cajun spice mix
- 1 tsp mustard
- 1 bell pepper, chopped
- ¼ cup vegetable broth
- Salt and black pepper, to taste

Directions:
1. Using a large saucepan with lightly salted water, place in asparagus and cook until tender for 10 minutes; drain. Set a wok over high heat and warm olive oil; stir in tofu cubes and cook for 6 minutes.
2. Place in garlic and cook for 30 seconds until soft. Stir in the rest of the ingredients, including reserved asparagus, and cook for an additional 4 minutes. Divide among plates and serve.

Nutrition:
- Info Per Servings 5.9g Carbs, 6.4g Protein, 8.9g Fat, 138 Calories

Cauliflower Fritters

Servings: 6
Cooking Time: 15 Minutes
Ingredients:
- 1 large cauliflower head, cut into florets
- 2 eggs, beaten
- ½ teaspoon turmeric
- 1 large onion, peeled and chopped
- ½ teaspoon salt
- ¼ teaspoon black pepper
- 6 tablespoons oil

Directions:
1. Place the cauliflower florets in a pot with water.
2. Bring to a boil and drain once cooked.
3. Place the cauliflower, eggs, onion, turmeric, salt, and pepper into the food processor.
4. Pulse until the mixture becomes coarse.
5. Transfer into a bowl. Using your hands, form six small flattened balls and place in the fridge for at least 1 hour until the mixture hardens.
6. Heat the oil in a skillet and fry the cauliflower patties for 3 minutes on each side.
7. Serve and enjoy.

Nutrition:
- Info Per Servings 2.28g Carbs, 3.9g Protein, 15.3g Fat, 157 Calories

Grated Cauliflower With Seasoned Mayo

Servings: 2
Cooking Time: 15 Mins
Ingredients:
- 1 lb grated cauliflower
- 3 oz. butter
- 4 eggs
- 3 oz. pimientos de padron or poblano peppers
- ½ cup mayonnaise
- 1 tsp olive oil
- Salt and pepper
- 1 tsp garlic powder (optional)

Directions:
1. In a bowl, whisk together the mayonnaise and garlic and set aside.
2. Rinse, trim and grate the cauliflower using a food processor or grater.
3. Melt a generous amount of butter and fry grated cauliflower for about 5 minutes. Season salt and pepper to taste.
4. Fry poblanos with oil until lightly crispy. Then fry eggs as you want and sprinkle salt and pepper over them.
5. Serve with poblanos and cauliflower. Drizzle some mayo mixture on top.

Nutrition:
- Info Per Servings 9g Carbs, 17g Protein, 87g Fat, 898 Calories

Vegan Mushroom Pizza

Servings: 4
Cooking Time: 35 Minutes
Ingredients:
- 2 tsp ghee
- 1 cup chopped button mushrooms
- ½ cup sliced mixed colored bell peppers
- Pink salt and black pepper to taste
- 1 almond flour pizza bread
- 1 cup tomato sauce
- 1 tsp vegan Parmesan cheese
- Vegan Parmesan cheese for garnish

Directions:
1. Melt ghee in a skillet over medium heat, sauté the mushrooms and bell peppers for 10 minutes to soften. Season with salt and black pepper. Turn the heat off.
2. Put the pizza bread on a pizza pan, spread the tomato sauce all over the top and scatter vegetables evenly on top. Season with a little more salt and sprinkle with parmesan cheese.
3. Bake for 20 minutes until the vegetables are soft and the cheese has melted and is bubbly. Garnish with extra parmesan cheese. Slice pizza and serve with chilled berry juice.

Nutrition:
- Info Per Servings 8g Carbs, 15g Protein, 20g Fat, 295 Calories

Cilantro-lime Guacamole

Servings: 4
Cooking Time: 10 Minutes
Ingredients:
- 3 avocados, peeled, pitted, and mashed
- 1 lime, juiced
- 1/2 cup diced onion
- 3 tablespoons chopped fresh cilantro
- 2 Roma (plum) tomatoes, diced
- 1 teaspoon salt
- 1 teaspoon minced garlic
- 1 pinch ground cayenne pepper (optional)
- 1 teaspoon minced garlic

Directions:
1. In a mixing bowl, mash the avocados with a fork. Sprinkle with salt and lime juice.
2. Stir together diced onion, tomatoes, cilantro, pepper and garlic.
3. Serve immediately, or refrigerate until ready to serve.

Nutrition:
- Info Per Servings 8g Carbs, 19g Protein, 22.2g Fat, 362 Calories

Easy Cauliflower Soup

Servings: 4
Cooking Time: 15 Minutes
Ingredients:
- 2 tbsp olive oil
- 2 onions, finely chopped
- 1 tsp garlic, minced
- 1 pound cauliflower, cut into florets
- 1 cup kale, chopped
- 4 cups vegetable broth
- ½ cup almond milk
- ½ tsp salt
- ½ tsp red pepper flakes
- 1 tbsp fresh chopped parsley

Directions:
1. Set a pot over medium-high heat and warm the oil. Add garlic and onion and sauté until browned and softened. Place in vegetable broth, kale, and cauliflower; cook for 10 minutes until the mixture boils. Stir in the pepper, salt, and almond milk; simmer the soup while covered for 5 minutes.
2. Transfer the soup to an immersion blender and blend to achieve the required consistency; top with parsley and serve immediately.

Nutrition:
- Info Per Servings 11.8g Carbs, 8.1g Protein, 10.3g Fat, 172 Calories

Stuffed Portobello Mushrooms

Servings: 2
Cooking Time: 30 Minutes
Ingredients:
- 4 portobello mushrooms, stems removed
- 2 tbsp olive oil
- 2 cups lettuce
- 1 cup crumbled blue cheese

Directions:
1. Preheat the oven to 350°F. Fill the mushrooms with blue cheese and place on a lined baking sheet; bake for 20 minutes. Serve with lettuce drizzled with olive oil.

Nutrition:
- Info Per Servings 5.5g Carbs, 14g Protein, 29g Fat, 334 Calories

Tomato Stuffed Avocado

Servings: 4
Cooking Time: 10 Minutes
Ingredients:
- 2 avocados, peeled and pitted
- 1 tomato, chopped
- ¼ cup walnuts, ground
- 2 carrots, chopped
- 1 garlic clove
- 1 tsp lemon juice
- 1 tbsp soy sauce
- Salt and black pepper, to taste

Directions:
1. Using a mixing bowl, mix soy sauce, carrots, avocado pulp, lemon juice, walnuts, and garlic.
2. Add pepper and salt. Plate the mixture into the avocado halves. Scatter walnuts over to serve.

Nutrition:
- Info Per Servings 5.5g Carbs, 3.5g Protein, 24.8g Fat, 263 Calories

Strawberry Mug Cake

Servings: 8
Cooking Time: 3 Mins
Ingredients:
- 2 slices fresh strawberry
- 1 teaspoon chia seeds
- 1 teaspoon poppy seeds
- What you'll need from the store cupboard:
- 1/4 teaspoon baking powder
- 3 leaves fresh mint
- 2 tablespoons cream of coconut

Directions:
1. Add all the ingredients together in a mug, stir until finely combined.
2. Cook in microwave at full power for 3 minutes then allow to cool before you serve.

Nutrition:
- Info Per Servings 4.7g Carbs, 2.4g Protein, 12g Fat, 196 Calories

Creamy Cucumber Avocado Soup

Servings: 4
Cooking Time: 15 Minutes
Ingredients:
- 4 large cucumbers, seeded, chopped
- 1 large avocado, peeled and pitted
- Salt and black pepper to taste
- 2 cups water
- 1 tbsp cilantro, chopped
- 3 tbsp olive oil
- 2 limes, juiced
- 2 tsp minced garlic
- 2 tomatoes, evenly chopped
- 1 chopped avocado for garnish

Directions:
1. Pour the cucumbers, avocado halves, salt, pepper, olive oil, lime juice, cilantro, water, and garlic in the food processor. Puree the ingredients for 2 minutes or until smooth.
2. Pour the mixture in a bowl and top with avocado and tomatoes. Serve chilled with zero-carb bread.

Nutrition:
- Info Per Servings 4.1g Carbs, 3.7g Protein, 7.4g Fat, 170 Calories

Greek Styled Veggie-rice

Servings: 3
Cooking Time: 20 Minutes
Ingredients:
- 3 tbsp chopped fresh mint
- 1 small tomato, chopped
- 1 head cauliflower, cut into large florets
- ¼ cup fresh lemon juice
- ½ yellow onion, minced
- pepper and salt to taste
- ¼ cup extra virgin olive oil

Directions:
1. In a bowl, mix lemon juice and onion and leave for 30 minutes. Then drain onion and reserve the juice and onion bits.
2. In a blender, shred cauliflower until the size of a grain of rice.
3. On medium fire, place a medium nonstick skillet and for 8-10 minutes cook cauliflower while covered.
4. Add grape tomatoes and cook for 3 minutes while stirring occasionally.
5. Add mint and onion bits. Cook for another three minutes.
6. Meanwhile, in a small bowl whisk pepper, salt, 3 tbsp reserved lemon juice, and olive oil until well blended.
7. Remove cooked cauliflower, transfer to a serving bowl, pour lemon juice mixture, and toss to mix.
8. Before serving, if needed season with pepper and salt to taste.

Nutrition:
- Info Per Servings 4.0g Carbs, 2.3g Protein, 9.5g Fat, 120 Calories

Greek-style Zucchini Pasta

Servings: 4
Cooking Time: 15 Minutes
Ingredients:
- ¼ cup sun-dried tomatoes
- 5 garlic cloves, minced
- 2 tbsp butter
- 1 cup spinach
- 2 large zucchinis, spiralized
- ¼ cup crumbled feta
- ¼ cup Parmesan cheese, shredded
- 10 kalamata olives, halved
- 2 tbsp olive oil
- 2 tbsp chopped parsley

Directions:
1. Heat the olive oil in a pan over medium heat. Add zoodles, butter, garlic, and spinach. Cook for about 5 minutes. Stir in the olives, tomatoes, and parsley. Cook for 2 more minutes. Add in the cheeses and serve.

Nutrition:
- Info Per Servings 6.5g Carbs, 6.5g Protein, 19.5g Fat, 231 Calories

Classic Tangy Ratatouille

Servings: 6
Cooking Time: 47 Minutes
Ingredients:
- 2 eggplants, chopped
- 3 zucchinis, chopped
- 2 red onions, diced
- 1 can tomatoes
- 2 red bell peppers, cut in chunks
- 1 yellow bell pepper, cut in chunks
- 3 cloves garlic, sliced
- ½ cup basil leaves, chop half
- 4 sprigs thyme
- 1 tbsp balsamic vinegar
- 2 tbsp olive oil
- ½ lemon, zested

Directions:
1. In a casserole pot, heat the olive oil and sauté the eggplants, zucchinis, and bell peppers over medium heat for 5 minutes. Spoon the veggies into a large bowl.
2. In the same pan, sauté garlic, onions, and thyme leaves for 5 minutes and return the cooked veggies to the pan along with the canned tomatoes, balsamic vinegar, chopped basil, salt, and pepper to taste. Stir and cover the pot, and cook the ingredients on low heat for 30 minutes.
3. Open the lid and stir in the remaining basil leaves, lemon zest, and adjust the seasoning. Turn the heat off. Plate the ratatouille and serve with some low carb crusted bread.

Nutrition:
- Info Per Servings 5.6g Carbs, 1.7g Protein, 12.1g Fat, 154 Calories

Pumpkin Bake

Servings: 6
Cooking Time: 45 Minutes
Ingredients:
- 3 large Pumpkins, peeled and sliced
- 1 cup almond flour
- 1 cup grated mozzarella cheese
- 2 tbsp olive oil
- ½ cup chopped parsley

Directions:
1. Preheat the oven to 350°F. Arrange the pumpkin slices in a baking dish, drizzle with olive oil, and bake for 35 minutes. Mix the almond flour, cheese, and parsley and when the pumpkin is ready, remove it from the oven, and sprinkle the cheese mixture all over. Place back in the oven and grill the top for 5 minutes.

Nutrition:
- Info Per Servings 5.7g Carbs, 2.7g Protein, 4.8g Fat, 125 Calories

Coconut Cauliflower Rice

Servings: 3
Cooking Time: 15 Minutes
Ingredients:
- 1 head cauliflower, grated
- ½ cup heavy cream
- ¼ cup butter, melted
- 3 cloves of garlic, minced
- 1 onion, chopped
- Salt and pepper to taste

Directions:
1. Place a nonstick saucepan on high fire and heat cream and butter.
2. Saute onion and garlic for 3 minutes.
3. Stir in grated cauliflower. Season with pepper and salt.
4. Cook until cauliflower is tender, around 5 minutes.
5. Turn off fire and let it set for 5 minutes.
6. Serve and enjoy.

Nutrition:
- Info Per Servings 9g Carbs, 3g Protein, 23g Fat, 246 Calories

Sauces And Dressing Recipes

Fat-burning Dressing

Servings: 6
Cooking Time: 3 Minutes
Ingredients:
- 2 tablespoons coconut oil
- ¼ cup olive oil
- 2 cloves of garlic, minced
- 2 tablespoons freshly chopped herbs of your choice
- ¼ cup mayonnaise
- Salt and pepper to taste

Directions:
1. Heat the coconut oil and olive oil and sauté the garlic until fragrant in a saucepan.
2. Allow cooling slightly before adding the mayonnaise.
3. Season with salt and pepper to taste.

Nutrition:
- Info Per Servings 0.6g Carbs, 14.1g Protein, 22.5g Fat, 262 Calories

Tzatziki

Servings: 4
Cooking Time: 10 Minutes, Plus At Least 30 Minutes To Chill
Ingredients:
- ½ large English cucumber, unpeeled
- 1½ cups Greek yogurt (I use Fage)
- 2 tablespoons olive oil
- Large pinch pink Himalayan salt
- Large pinch freshly ground black pepper
- Juice of ½ lemon
- 2 garlic cloves, finely minced
- 1 tablespoon fresh dill

Directions:
1. Halve the cucumber lengthwise, and use a spoon to scoop out and discard the seeds.
2. Grate the cucumber with a zester or grater onto a large plate lined with a few layers of paper towels. Close the paper towels around the grated cucumber, and squeeze as much water out of it as you can. (This can take a while and can require multiple paper towels. You can also allow it to drain overnight in a strainer or wrapped in a few layers of cheesecloth in the fridge if you have the time.)
3. In a food processor (or blender), blend the yogurt, olive oil, pink Himalayan salt, pepper, lemon juice, and garlic until fully combined.
4. Transfer the mixture to a medium bowl, and mix in the fresh dill and grated cucumber.
5. I like to chill this sauce for at least 30 minutes before serving. Keep in a sealed glass container in the refrigerator for up to 1 week.

Nutrition:
- Info Per Servings 5g Carbs, 8g Protein, 11g Fat, 149 Calories

Caesar Dressing

Servings: 4
Cooking Time: 5 Minutes
Ingredients:
- ½ cup mayonnaise
- 1 tablespoon Dijon mustard
- Juice of ½ lemon
- ½ teaspoon Worcestershire sauce
- Pinch pink Himalayan salt
- Pinch freshly ground black pepper
- ¼ cup grated Parmesan cheese

Directions:
1. In a medium bowl, whisk together the mayonnaise, mustard, lemon juice, Worcestershire sauce, pink Himalayan salt, and pepper until fully combined.
2. Add the Parmesan cheese, and whisk until creamy and well blended.
3. Keep in a sealed glass container in the refrigerator for up to 1 week.

Nutrition:
- Info Per Servings Calories: 2g Carbs, 2g Protein, 23g Fat, 222 Calories

Chunky Blue Cheese Dressing

Servings: 4
Cooking Time: 5 Minutes
Ingredients:
- ½ cup sour cream
- ½ cup mayonnaise
- Juice of ½ lemon
- ½ teaspoon Worcestershire sauce
- Pink Himalayan salt
- Freshly ground black pepper
- 2 ounces crumbled blue cheese

Directions:
1. In a medium bowl, whisk the sour cream, mayonnaise, lemon juice, and Worcestershire sauce. Season with pink Himalayan salt and pepper, and whisk again until fully combined.
2. Fold in the crumbled blue cheese until well combined.
3. Keep in a sealed glass container in the refrigerator for up to 1 week.

Nutrition:
- Info Per Servings 3g Carbs, 7g Protein, 32g Fat, 306 Calories

Avocado Mayo

Servings: 4
Cooking Time: 5 Minutes
Ingredients:
- 1 medium avocado, cut into chunks
- ½ teaspoon ground cayenne pepper
- Juice of ½ lime
- 2 tablespoons fresh cilantro leaves (optional)
- Pinch pink Himalayan salt
- ¼ cup olive oil

Directions:
1. In a food processor (or blender), blend the avocado, cayenne pepper, lime juice, cilantro, and pink Himalayan salt until all the ingredients are well combined and smooth.
2. Slowly incorporate the olive oil, adding 1 tablespoon at a time, pulsing the food processor in between.
3. Keep in a sealed glass container in the refrigerator for up to 1 week.

Nutrition:
- Info Per Servings 1g Carbs, 1g Protein, 5g Fat, 58 Calories

Vegetarian Fish Sauce

Servings: 16
Cooking Time: 20 Minutes

Ingredients:
- 1/4 cup dried shiitake mushrooms
- 1-2 tbsp tamari (for a depth of flavor)
- 3 tbsp coconut aminos
- 1 ¼ cup water
- 2 tsp sea salt

Directions:
1. To a small saucepan, add water, coconut aminos, dried shiitake mushrooms, and sea salt. Bring to a boil, then cover, reduce heat, and simmer for 15-20 minutes.
2. Remove from heat and let cool slightly. Pour liquid through a fine-mesh strainer into a bowl, pressing on the mushroom mixture with a spoon to squeeze out any remaining liquid.
3. To the bowl, add tamari. Taste and adjust as needed, adding more sea salt for saltiness.
4. Store in a sealed container in the refrigerator for up to 1 month and shake well before use. Or pour into an ice cube tray, freeze, and store in a freezer-safe container for up to 2 months.

Nutrition:
- Info Per Servings 5g Carbs, 0.3g Protein, 2g Fat, 39.1 Calories

Celery-onion Vinaigrette

Servings: 4
Cooking Time: 0 Minutes

Ingredients:
- 1 tbsp finely chopped celery
- 1 tbsp finely chopped red onion
- 4 garlic cloves, minced
- ½ cup red wine vinegar
- 1 tbsp extra virgin olive oil

Directions:
1. Prepare the dressing by mixing pepper, celery, onion, olive oil, garlic, and vinegar in a small bowl. Whisk well to combine.
2. Let it sit for at least 30 minutes to let flavors blend.
3. Serve and enjoy with your favorite salad greens.

Nutrition:
- Info Per Servings 1.4g Carbs, 0.2g Protein, 3.4g Fat, 41 Calories

Fish And Seafood Recipes

Steamed Herbed Red Snapper

Servings: 4
Cooking Time: 15 Minutes
Ingredients:
- 4 red snapper fillets
- ¼ tsp. paprika
- 3 tbsp. lemon juice, freshly squeezed
- 1 ½ tsp chopped fresh herbs of your choice (rosemary, thyme, basil, or parsley)
- 6 tbsp olive oil
- Salt and pepper to taste

Directions:
1. In a small bowl, whisk well paprika, lemon juice, olive oil, and herbs. Season with pepper and salt.
2. Place a trivet in a large saucepan and pour a cup or two of water into the pan. Bring to a boil.
3. Place snapper in a heatproof dish that fits inside a saucepan. Season snapper with pepper and salt. Drizzle with lemon mixture.
4. Seal dish with foil. Place the dish on the trivet inside the saucepan. Cover and steam for 15 minutes.
5. Serve and enjoy.

Nutrition:
- Info Per Servings 2.1g Carbs, 45.6g Protein, 20.3g Fat, 374 Calories

Chipotle Salmon Asparagus

Servings: 2
Cooking Time: 15 Minutes
Ingredients:
- 1-lb salmon fillet, skin on
- 2 teaspoon chipotle paste
- A handful of asparagus spears, trimmed
- 1 lemon, sliced thinly
- A pinch of rosemary
- Salt to taste
- 5 tbsp olive oil

Directions:
1. In a heat-proof dish that fits inside the saucepan, add asparagus spears on the bottom of the dish. Place fish, top with rosemary, and lemon slices. Season with chipotle paste and salt. Drizzle with olive oil. Cover dish with foil.
2. Place a large saucepan on the medium-high fire. Place a trivet inside the saucepan and fill the pan halfway with water. Cover and bring to a boil.
3. Place dish on the trivet.
4. Cover pan and steam for 10 minutes. Let it rest in pan for another 5 minutes.
5. Serve and enjoy topped with pepper.

Nutrition:
- Info Per Servings 2.8g Carbs, 35.0g Protein, 50.7g Fat, 651 Calories

Coconut Crab Patties

Servings: 8
Cooking Time: 15 Minutes
Ingredients:
- 2 tbsp coconut oil
- 1 tbsp lemon juice
- 1 cup lump crab meat
- 2 tsp Dijon mustard
- 1 egg, beaten
- 1 ½ tbsp coconut flour

Directions:
1. In a bowl to the crabmeat add all the ingredients, except for the oil; mix well to combine. Make patties out of the mixture. Melt the coconut oil in a skillet over medium heat. Add the crab patties and cook for about 2-3 minutes per side.

Nutrition:
- Info Per Servings 3.6g Carbs, 15.3g Protein, 11.5g Fat, 215 Calories

Baked Cod And Tomato Capers Mix

Serves: 4
Cooking Time: 25 Minutes
Ingredients:
- 4 cod fillets, boneless
- 2 tablespoons avocado oil
- 1 cup tomato passata
- 2 tablespoons capers, drained
- 2 tablespoons parsley, choppedA pinch of salt and black pepper

Directions:
1. In a roasting pan, combine the cod with the oil and the other ingredients, toss gently, introduce in the oven at 370 °F and bake for 25 minutes.
2. Divide between plates and serve.

Nutrition:
- 0.7g carbs; 2g fat; 5g protein; 150 calories

Spicy Sea Bass With Hazelnuts

Servings: 2
Cooking Time: 30 Minutes
Ingredients:
- 2 sea bass fillets
- 2 tbsp butter
- ⅓ cup roasted hazelnuts
- A pinch of cayenne pepper

Directions:
1. Preheat your oven to 425 °F. Line a baking dish with waxed paper. Melt the butter and brush it over the fish. In a food processor, combine the rest of the ingredients. Coat the sea bass with the hazelnut mixture. Place in the oven and bake for about 15 minutes.

Nutrition:
- Info Per Servings 2.8g Carbs, 40g Protein, 31g Fat, 467 Calories

Lemon Chili Halibut

Servings: 2
Cooking Time: 15 Minutes
Ingredients:
- 1-lb halibut fillets
- 1 lemon, sliced
- 1 tablespoon chili pepper flakes
- Pepper and salt to taste
- 4 tbsp olive oil

Directions:
1. In a heat-proof dish that fits inside saucepan, place fish. Top fish with chili flakes, lemon slices, salt, and pepper. Drizzle with olive oil. Cover dish with foil
2. Place a large saucepan on the medium-high fire. Place a trivet inside the saucepan and fill the pan halfway with water. Cover and bring to a boil.
3. Place dish on the trivet.
4. Cover pan and steam for 10 minutes. Let it rest in pan for another 5 minutes.
5. Serve and enjoy topped with pepper.

Nutrition:
- Info Per Servings 4.2g Carbs, 42.7g Protein, 58.4g Fat, 675 Calories

Shrimp In Curry Sauce

Servings: 2
Cooking Time: 25 Minutes
Ingredients:
- ½ ounces grated Parmesan cheese
- 1 tbsp water
- 1 egg, beaten
- ¼ tsp curry powder
- 2 tsp almond flour
- 12 shrimp, shelled
- 3 tbsp coconut oil
- Sauce
- 2 tbsp curry leaves
- 2 tbsp butter
- ½ onion, diced
- ½ cup heavy cream
- ½ ounce cheddar

Directions:
1. Combine all dry ingredients for the batter. Melt the coconut oil in a skillet over medium heat. Dip the shrimp in the egg first, and then coat with the dry mixture. Fry until golden and crispy.
2. In another skillet, melt the butter. Add onion and cook for 3 minutes. Add curry leaves and cook for 30 seconds. Stir in heavy cream and cheddar and cook until thickened. Add the shrimp and coat well. Serve warm.

Nutrition:
- Info Per Servings 4.3g Carbs, 24.4g Protein, 41g Fat, 560 Calories

Simply Steamed Alaskan Cod

Servings: 2
Cooking Time: 15 Minutes
Ingredients:
- 1-lb fillet wild Alaskan Cod
- 1 cup cherry tomatoes, halved
- 1 tbsp balsamic vinegar
- 1 tbsp fresh basil chopped
- Salt and pepper to taste
- 5 tbsp olive oil

Directions:
1. In a heat-proof dish that fits inside the saucepan, add all ingredients except for basil. Mix well.
2. Place a large saucepan on the medium-high fire. Place a trivet inside the saucepan and fill pan halfway with water. Cover and bring to a boil.
3. Cover dish with foil and place on a trivet.
4. Cover pan and steam for 10 minutes. Let it rest in pan for another 5 minutes.
5. Serve and enjoy topped with fresh basil.

Nutrition:
- Info Per Servings 4.2g Carbs, 41.0g Protein, 36.6g Fat, 495.2 Calories

Golden Pompano In Microwave

Servings: 2
Cooking Time: 11 Minutes
Ingredients:
- ½-lb pompano
- 1 tbsp soy sauce, low sodium
- 1-inch thumb ginger, diced
- 1 lemon, halved
- 1 stalk green onions, chopped
- ¼ cup water
- 1 tsp pepper
- 4 tbsp olive oil

Directions:
1. In a microwavable casserole dish, mix well all ingredients except for pompano, green onions, and lemon.
2. Squeeze half of the lemon in dish and slice into thin circles the other half.
3. Place pompano in the dish and add lemon circles on top of the fish. Drizzle with pepper and olive oil.
4. Cover top of a casserole dish with a microwave-safe plate.
5. Microwave for 5 minutes.
6. Remove from microwave, turn over fish, sprinkle green onions, top with a microwavable plate.
7. Return to microwave and cook for another 3 minutes.
8. Let it rest for 3 minutes more.
9. Serve and enjoy.

Nutrition:
- Info Per Servings 6.3g Carbs, 22.2g Protein, 39.5g Fat, 464 Calories

Steamed Asparagus And Shrimps

Servings: 6
Cooking Time: 15 Minutes
Ingredients:
- 1-pound shrimps, peeled and deveined
- 1 bunch asparagus, trimmed
- ½ tablespoon Cajun seasoning
- 2 tablespoons butter
- 5 tablespoons oil
- Salt and pepper to taste

Directions:
1. In a heat-proof dish that fits inside the saucepan, add all ingredients. Mix well.
2. Place a large saucepan on the medium-high fire. Place a trivet inside the saucepan and fill the pan halfway with water. Cover and bring to a boil.
3. Cover dish with foil and place on a trivet.
4. Cover pan and steam for 10 minutes. Let it rest in pan for another 5 minutes.
5. Serve and enjoy.

Nutrition:
- Info Per Servings 1.1g Carbs, 15.5g Protein, 15.8g Fat, 204.8 Calories

Avocado Salad With Shrimp

Serves: 4
Cooking Time: 10 Minutes
Ingredients:
- 2 tomatoes, sliced into cubes
- 2 medium avocados, cut into large pieces
- 3 tablespoons red onion, diced
- ½ large lettuce, chopped
- 2 lbs. shrimp, peeled and deveined
- For the Lime Vinaigrette Dressing
- 2 cloves garlic, minced
- 1 ½ teaspoon Dijon mustard
- 1/3 cup extra virgin olive oil
- salt and pepper to taste
- 1/3 cup lime juice

Directions:
1. Add the peeled and deveined shrimp and 2 quarts of water to a cooking pot and print to a boil, lower the heat and let them simmer for 1-2 minutes until the shrimp is pink. Set aside and let them cool.
2. Next add the chopped lettuce in a large bowl. Then add the avocado, tomatoes, shrimp and red onion.
3. In a small bowl whisk together the Dijon mustard, garlic, olive oil and lime juice. Mix well.
4. Pour the lime vinaigrette dressing over the salad and serve.

Nutrition:
- Per serving: 7g Carbs; 43.5g Protein; 17.6g Fat; 377 Calories;

Avocado And Salmon

Serves: 2
Cooking Time: 0 Minutes
Ingredients:
- 1 avocado, halved, pitted
- 2 oz flaked salmon, packed in water
- 1 tbsp mayonnaise
- 1 tbsp grated cheddar cheese
- Seasoning:
- 1/8 tsp salt
- 2 tbsp coconut oil

Directions:
1. Prepare the avocado and for this, cut avocado in half and then remove its seed. Drain the salmon, add it in a bowl along with remaining ingredients, stir well and then scoop into the hollow on an avocado half. Serve.

Nutrition:
- 3 g Carbs; 19 g Protein; 48 g Fats; 525 Calories

Grilled Shrimp With Chimichurri Sauce

Servings: 4
Cooking Time: 55 Minutes
Ingredients:
- 1 pound shrimp, peeled and deveined
- 2 tbsp olive oil
- Juice of 1 lime
- Chimichurri
- ½ tsp salt
- ¼ cup olive oil
- 2 garlic cloves
- ¼ cup red onion, chopped
- ¼ cup red wine vinegar
- ½ tsp pepper
- 2 cups parsley
- ¼ tsp red pepper flakes

Directions:
1. Process the chimichurri ingredients in a blender until smooth; set aside. Combine shrimp, olive oil, and lime juice, in a bowl, and let marinate in the fridge for 30 minutes. Preheat your grill to medium. Add shrimp and cook about 2 minutes per side. Serve shrimp drizzled with the chimichurri sauce.

Nutrition:
- Info Per Servings 3.5g Carbs, 16g Protein, 20.3g Fat, 283 Calories

Steamed Mustard Salmon

Servings: 4
Cooking Time: 15 Minutes
Ingredients:
- 2 tbsp Dijon mustard
- 1 whole lemon
- 2 cloves of garlic, minced
- 4 salmon fillets, skin removed
- 1 tbsp dill weed
- Salt and pepper to taste

Directions:
1. Slice lemon in half. Slice one lemon in circles and juice the other half in a small bowl.
2. Whisk in mustard, garlic, and dill weed in a bowl of lemon. Season with pepper and salt.
3. Place a trivet in a large saucepan and pour a cup or two of water into the pan. Bring to a boil.
4. Place lemon slices in a heatproof dish that fits inside a saucepan. Season salmon with pepper and salt. Slather mustard mixture on top of salmon.
5. Seal dish with foil. Place the dish on the trivet inside the saucepan. Cover and steam for 15 minutes.
6. Serve and enjoy.

Nutrition:
- Info Per Servings 2.2g Carbs, 65.3g Protein, 14.8g Fat, 402 Calories

Lemon Marinated Salmon With Spices

Servings: 2
Cooking Time: 15 Minutes
Ingredients:
- 2 tablespoons. lemon juice
- 1 tablespoon. yellow miso paste
- 2 teaspoons. Dijon mustard
- 1 pinch cayenne pepper and sea salt to taste
- 2 center-cut salmon fillets, boned; skin on
- 1 1/2 tablespoons mayonnaise
- 1 tablespoon ground black pepper

Directions:
1. In a bowl, combine lemon juice with black pepper. Stir in mayonnaise, miso paste, Dijon mustard, and cayenne pepper, mix well. Pour over salmon fillets, reserve about a tablespoon marinade. Cover and marinate the fish in the refrigerator for 30 minutes.
2. Preheat oven to 450 degrees F. Line a baking sheet with parchment paper.
3. Lay fillets on the prepared baking sheet. Rub the reserved lemon-pepper marinade on fillets. Then season with cayenne pepper and sea salt to taste.
4. Bake in the oven for 10 to 15 minutes until cooked through.

Nutrition:
- Info Per Servings 7.1g Carbs, 20g Protein, 28.1g Fat, 361 Calories

Chili-lime Shrimps

Servings: 4
Cooking Time: 10 Minutes
Ingredients:
- 1 ½ lb. raw shrimp, peeled and deveined
- 1 tbsp. chili flakes
- 5 tbsp sweet chili sauce
- 2 tbsp. lime juice, freshly squeezed
- 1 tsp cayenne pepper
- Salt and pepper to taste
- 5 tbsp oil
- 3 tbsp water

Directions:
1. In a small bowl, whisk well chili flakes, sweet chili sauce, cayenne pepper, and water.
2. On medium-high fire, heat a nonstick saucepan for 2 minutes. Add oil to a pan and swirl to coat bottom and sides. Heat oil for a minute.
3. Stir fry shrimp, around 5 minutes. Season lightly with salt and pepper.
4. Stir in sweet chili mixture and toss well shrimp to coat.
5. Turn off fire, drizzle lime juice and toss well to coat.
6. Serve and enjoy.

Nutrition:
- Info Per Servings 1.7g Carbs, 34.9g Protein, 19.8g Fat, 306 Calories

Air Fryer Seasoned Salmon Fillets

Servings: 4
Cooking Time: 10 Mins
Ingredients:
- 2 lbs. salmon fillets
- 1 tsp. stevia
- 2 tbsp. whole grain mustard
- 1 clove of garlic, minced
- 1/2 tsp. thyme leaves
- 2 tsp. extra-virgin olive oil
- Cooking spray
- Salt and black pepper to taste

Directions:
1. Preheat your Air Fryer to 390 degrees F.
2. Season salmon fillets with salt and pepper.
3. Add together the mustard, garlic, stevia, thyme, and oil in a bowl, stir to combined well. Rub the seasoning mixture on top of salmon fillets.
4. Spray the Air Fryer basket with cooking spray and cook seasoned fillets for 10 minutes until crispy. Let it cool before serving.

Nutrition:
- Info Per Servings 14g Carbs, 18g Protein, 10g Fat, 238 Calories

Bang Bang Shrimps

Serves: 2
Cooking Time: 6 Minutes
Ingredients:
- 4 oz shrimps¼ tsp paprika
- ¼ tsp apple cider vinegar
- 2 tbsp sweet chili sauce
- ¼ cup mayonnaise
- Seasoning:
- ¼ tsp salt
- 1/8 tsp ground black pepper
- 2 tsp avocado oil

Directions:
1. Take a medium skillet pan, place it over medium heat, add oil and wait until it gets hot. Season shrimps with salt, black pepper, and paprika until coated, add them to the pan, and cook for 2 to 3 minutes per side until pink and cooked. Take a medium bowl, place mayonnaise in it, and then whisk in vinegar and chili sauce until combined. Add shrimps into the mayonnaise mixture, toss until coated, and then serve.

Nutrition:
- 7.2 g Carbs; 13 g Protein; 23.1 g Fats; 290 Calories

Blackened Fish Tacos With Slaw

Servings: 4
Cooking Time: 20 Minutes
Ingredients:
- 1 tbsp olive oil
- 1 tsp chili powder
- 2 tilapia fillets
- 1 tsp paprika
- 4 low carb tortillas
- Slaw:
- ½ cup red cabbage, shredded
- 1 tbsp lemon juice
- 1 tsp apple cider vinegar
- 1 tbsp olive oil

Directions:
1. Season the tilapia with chili powder and paprika. Heat the olive oil in a skillet over medium heat.
2. Add tilapia and cook until blackened, about 3 minutes per side. Cut into strips. Divide the tilapia between the tortillas. Combine all slaw ingredients in a bowl. Split the slaw among the tortillas.

Nutrition:
- Info Per Servings 3.5g Carbs, 13.8g Protein, 20g Fat, 268 Calories

Poultry Recipes

Chicken, Broccoli & Cashew Stir-fry

Servings: 4
Cooking Time: 30 Minutes
Ingredients:
- 2 chicken breasts, cut into strips
- 3 tbsp olive oil
- 2 tbsp soy sauce
- 2 tsp white wine vinegar
- 1 tsp erythritol
- 2 tsp xanthan gum
- 1 lemon, juiced
- 1 cup unsalted cashew nuts
- 2 cups broccoli florets
- 1 white onion, thinly sliced
- Pepper to taste

Directions:
1. In a bowl, mix the soy sauce, vinegar, lemon juice, erythritol, and xanthan gum. Set aside.
2. Heat the oil in a wok and fry the cashew for 4 minutes until golden-brown. Remove the cashews into a paper towel lined plate and set aside. Sauté the onion in the same oil for 4 minutes until soft and browned; add to the cashew nuts.
3. Add the chicken to the wok and cook for 4 minutes; include the broccoli and pepper. Stir-fry and pour the soy sauce mixture in. Stir and cook the sauce for 4 minutes and pour in the cashews and onion. Stir once more, cook for 1 minute, and turn the heat off.
4. Serve the chicken stir-fry with some steamed cauli rice.

Nutrition:
- Info Per Servings 3.4g Carbs, 17.3g Protein, 10.1g Fat, 286 Calories

Bacon & Cheese Chicken

Servings: 4
Cooking Time: 30 Minutes
Ingredients:
- 4 bacon strips
- 4 chicken breasts
- 3 green onions, chopped
- 4 ounces ranch dressing
- 1 ounce coconut aminos
- 2 tbsp coconut oil
- 4 oz Monterey Jack cheese, grated

Directions:
1. Set a pan over high heat and warm the oil. Place in the chicken breasts, cook for 7 minutes, then flip to the other side; cook for an additional 7 minutes. Set another pan over medium-high heat, place in the bacon, cook until crispy, remove to paper towels, drain the grease, and crumble.
2. Add the chicken breast to a baking dish. Place the green onions, coconut aminos, cheese, and crumbled bacon on top, set in an oven, turn on the broiler, and cook for 5 minutes at high temperature. Split among serving plates and serve.

Nutrition:
- Info Per Servings 3.3g Carbs, 34g Protein, 21g Fat, 423 Calories

Chicken Goujons With Tomato Sauce

Servings: 8
Cooking Time: 50 Minutes
Ingredients:
- 1½ pounds chicken breasts, skinless, boneless, cubed
- Salt and ground black pepper, to taste
- 1 egg
- 1 cup almond flour
- ¼ cup Parmesan cheese, grated
- ½ tsp garlic powder
- 1½ tsp dried parsley
- ½ tsp dried basil
- 4 tbsp avocado oil
- 4 cups spaghetti squash, cooked
- 6 oz gruyere cheese, shredded
- 1½ cups tomato sauce
- Fresh basil, chopped, for serving

Directions:
1. Using a bowl, combine the almond flour with 1 teaspoon parsley, Parmesan cheese, pepper, garlic powder, and salt. In a separate bowl, combine the egg with pepper and salt. Dip the chicken in the egg, and then in almond flour mixture.
2. Set a pan over medium-high heat and warm 3 tablespoons avocado oil, add in the chicken, cook until golden, and remove to paper towels. Using a bowl, combine the spaghetti squash with salt, dried basil, rest of the parsley, 1 tablespoon avocado oil, and pepper.
3. Sprinkle this into a baking dish, top with the chicken pieces, followed by the marinara sauce. Scatter shredded gruyere cheese on top, and bake for 30 minutes at 360°F. Remove, and sprinkle with fresh basil before serving.

Nutrition:
- Info Per Servings 5g Carbs, 28g Protein, 36g Fat, 415 Calories

Lemon Threaded Chicken Skewers

Servings: 4
Cooking Time: 2 Hours 17 Minutes
Ingredients:
- 3 chicken breasts, cut into cubes
- 2 tbsp olive oil, divided
- 2/3 jar preserved lemon, flesh removed, drained
- 2 cloves garlic, minced
- ½ cup lemon juice
- Salt and black pepper to taste
- 1 tsp rosemary leaves to garnish
- 2 to 4 lemon wedges to garnish

Directions:
1. First, thread the chicken onto skewers and set aside.
2. In a wide bowl, mix half of the oil, garlic, salt, pepper, and lemon juice, and add the chicken skewers, and lemon rind. Cover the bowl and let the chicken marinate for at least 2 hours in the refrigerator.
3. When the marinating time is almost over, preheat a grill to 350°F, and remove the chicken onto the grill. Cook for 6 minutes on each side.
4. Remove and serve warm garnished with rosemary leaves and lemons wedges.

Nutrition:
- Info Per Servings 3.5g Carbs, 34g Protein, 11g Fat, 350 Calories

Chili Lime Chicken

Servings: 5
Cooking Time: 30 Minutes
Ingredients:
- 1 lb. chicken breasts, skin and bones removed
- Juice from 1 ½ limes, freshly squeezed
- 1 tbsp. chili powder
- 1 tsp. cumin
- 6 cloves garlic, minced
- Pepper and salt to taste
- 1 cup water
- 4 tablespoon olive oil

Directions:
1. Place all ingredients in a heavy-bottomed pot and give a good stir.
2. Place on high fire and bring it to a boil. Cover, lower fire to a simmer, and cook for 20 minutes.
3. Remove chicken and place in a bowl. Shred using two forks. Return shredded chicken to the pot.
4. Boil for 10 minutes or until sauce is rendered.
5. Serve and enjoy.

Nutrition:
- Info Per Servings 1.5g Carbs, 19.3g Protein, 19.5g Fat, 265 Calories

Parmesan Wings With Yogurt Sauce

Servings: 6
Cooking Time: 25 Minutes
Ingredients:
- For the Dipping Sauce
- 1 cup plain yogurt
- 1 tsp fresh lemon juice
- Salt and black pepper to taste
- For the Wings
- 2 lb chicken wings
- Salt and black pepper to taste
- Cooking spray
- ½ cup melted butter
- ½ cup Hot sauce
- ¼ cup grated Parmesan cheese

Directions:
1. Mix the yogurt, lemon juice, salt, and black pepper in a bowl. Chill while making the chicken.
2. Preheat oven to 400°F and season wings with salt and black pepper. Line them on a baking sheet and grease lightly with cooking spray. Bake for 20 minutes until golden brown. Mix butter, hot sauce, and parmesan in a bowl. Toss chicken in the sauce to evenly coat and plate. Serve with yogurt dipping sauce and celery strips.

Nutrition:
- Info Per Servings 4g Carbs, 24g Protein, 36.4g Fat, 452 Calories

Chili Turkey Patties With Cucumber Salsa

Servings: 4
Cooking Time: 30 Minutes
Ingredients:
- 2 spring onions, thinly sliced
- 1 pound ground turkey
- 1 egg
- 2 garlic cloves, minced
- 1 tbsp chopped herbs
- 1 small chili pepper, deseeded and diced
- 2 tbsp ghee
- Cucumber Salsa
- 1 tbsp apple cider vinegar
- 1 tbsp chopped dill
- 1 garlic clove, minced
- 2 cucumbers, grated
- 1 cup sour cream
- 1 jalapeño pepper, minced
- 2 tbsp olive oil

Directions:
1. Place all turkey ingredients, except the ghee, in a bowl. Mix to combine. Make patties out of the mixture. Melt the ghee in a skillet over medium heat. Cook the patties for 3 minutes per side.
2. Place all salsa ingredients in a bowl and mix to combine. Serve the patties topped with salsa.

Nutrition:
- Info Per Servings 5g Carbs, 26g Protein, 38g Fat, 475 Calories

Stir Fried Broccoli 'n Chicken

Servings: 5
Cooking Time: 20 Minutes
Ingredients:
- 1 tbsp. coconut oil
- 3 cloves of garlic, minced
- 1 ½ lb. chicken breasts, cut into strips
- ¼ cup coconut aminos
- 1 head broccoli, cut into florets
- Pepper to taste

Directions:
1. On medium fire, heat a saucepan for 2 minutes. Add oil to the pan and swirl to coat bottom and sides. Heat oil for a minute.
2. Add garlic and sauté for a minute. Stir in chicken and stir fry for 5 minutes.
3. Add remaining ingredients. Season generously with pepper.
4. Increase fire to high and stir fry for 3 minutes.
5. Lower fire to low, cover, and cook for 5 minutes.
6. Serve and enjoy.

Nutrition:
- Info Per Servings 1.8g Carbs, 28.6g Protein, 15.4g Fat, 263 Calories

Chicken Country Style

Servings: 4
Cooking Time: 25 Minutes
Ingredients:
- 3 tablespoons butter
- 1 packet dry Lipton's onion soup mix
- 1 can Campbell's chicken gravy
- 4 skinless and boneless chicken breasts
- 1/3 teaspoon pepper
- 1 cup water

Directions:
1. Add all ingredients in a pot on high fire and bring it to a boil.
2. Once boiling, lower fire to a simmer and cook for 25 minutes.
3. Adjust seasoning to taste.
4. Serve and enjoy.

Nutrition:
- Info Per Servings 6.8g Carbs, 53.7g Protein, 16.9g Fat, 380 Calories

Turkey Breast Salad

Servings: 4
Cooking Time: 25 Minutes
Ingredients:
- 1 tbsp swerve
- 1 red onion, chopped
- ¼ cup vinegar
- ¼ cup olive oil
- ¼ cup water
- 1¾ cups raspberries
- 1 tbsp Dijon mustard
- Salt and ground black pepper, to taste
- 10 ounces baby spinach
- 2 medium turkey breasts, boneless
- 4 ounces goat cheese, crumbled
- ½ cup pecans halves

Directions:
1. Using a blender, combine swerve, vinegar, 1 cup raspberries, pepper, mustard, water, onion, oil, and salt, and ensure well blended. Strain this into a bowl, and set aside. Cut the turkey breast in half, add a seasoning of pepper and salt, and place skin side down into a pan.
2. Cook for 8 minutes flipping to the other side and cooking for 5 minutes. Split the spinach among plates, spread with the remaining raspberries, pecan halves, and goat cheese. Slice the turkey breasts, put over the salad and top with raspberries vinaigrette and enjoy.

Nutrition:
- Info Per Servings 6g Carbs, 28g Protein, 33g Fat, 451 Calories

Baked Chicken Pesto

Servings: 4
Cooking Time: 20 Minutes

Ingredients:
- 2 tsp grated parmesan cheese
- 6 tbsp shredded reduced-fat mozzarella cheese
- 1 medium tomato (thinly sliced)
- 4 tsp basil pesto
- 2 boneless, skinless chicken breasts around 1-lb
- Salt and pepper to taste

Directions:
1. In cool water, wash chicken and dry using a paper towel. Create 4 thin slices of chicken breasts by slicing horizontally.
2. Preheat oven to 400oF and then line a baking sheet with parchment or foil.
3. Put into the baking sheet the slices of chicken. Season with pepper and salt. And spread at least 1 teaspoon of pesto on each chicken slice.
4. For 15 minutes, bake the chicken and ensure that the center is no longer pink. After which remove baking sheet and top chicken with parmesan cheese, mozzarella, and tomatoes.
5. Put into the oven once again and heat for another 3 to 5 minutes to melt the cheese, then ready to serve.

Nutrition:
- Info Per Servings 2.0g Carbs, 40.0g Protein, 8.0g Fat, 238 Calories

Greek Chicken With Capers

Servings: 4
Cooking Time: 30 Minutes

Ingredients:
- ¼ cup olive oil
- 1 onion, chopped
- 4 chicken breasts, skinless and boneless
- 4 garlic cloves, minced
- Salt and ground black pepper, to taste
- ½ cup kalamata olives, pitted and chopped
- 1 tbsp capers
- 1 pound tomatoes, chopped
- ½ tsp red chili flakes

Directions:
1. Sprinkle pepper and salt on the chicken, and rub with half of the oil. Add the chicken to a pan set over high heat, cook for 2 minutes, flip to the other side, and cook for 2 more minutes. Set the chicken breasts in the oven at 450°F and bake for 8 minutes. Split the chicken into serving plates.
2. Set the same pan over medium heat and warm the remaining oil, place in the onion, olives, capers, garlic, and chili flakes, and cook for 1 minute. Stir in the tomatoes, pepper, and salt, and cook for 2 minutes. Sprinkle over the chicken breasts and enjoy.

Nutrition:
- Info Per Servings 2.2g Carbs, 25g Protein, 21g Fat, 387 Calories

Thyme Chicken Thighs

Servings: 4
Cooking Time: 30 Minutes
Ingredients:
- ½ cup chicken stock
- 1 tbsp olive oil
- ½ cup chopped onion
- 4 chicken thighs
- ¼ cup heavy cream
- 2 tbsp Dijon mustard
- 1 tsp thyme
- 1 tsp garlic powder

Directions:
1. Heat the olive oil in a pan. Cook the chicken for about 4 minutes per side. Set aside. Sauté the onion in the same pan for 3 minutes, add the stock, and simmer for 5 minutes. Stir in mustard and heavy cream, along with thyme and garlic powder. Pour the sauce over the chicken and serve.

Nutrition:
- Info Per Servings 4g Carbs, 33g Protein, 42g Fat, 528 Calories

Chicken Stew With Sun-dried Tomatoes

Servings: 4
Cooking Time: 60 Minutes
Ingredients:
- 2 carrots, chopped
- 2 tbsp olive oil
- 2 celery stalks, chopped
- 2 cups chicken stock
- 1 shallot, chopped
- 28 oz chicken thighs, skinless, boneless
- 3 garlic cloves, peeled and minced
- ½ tsp dried rosemary
- 2 oz sun-dried tomatoes, chopped
- 1 cup spinach
- ¼ tsp dried thyme
- ½ cup heavy cream
- Salt and ground black pepper, to taste
- A pinch of xanthan gum

Directions:
1. In a pot, heat the olive oil over medium heat and add garlic, carrots, celery, and shallot; season with salt and pepper and sauté for 5-6 minutes until tender. Stir in the chicken and cook for 5 minutes.
2. Pour in the stock, tomatoes, rosemary, and thyme, and cook for 30 minutes covered. Stir in xanthan gum, cream, and spinach; cook for 5 minutes. Adjust the seasonings and separate into bowls.

Nutrition:
- Info Per Servings 6g Carbs, 23g Protein, 11g Fat, 224 Calories

Turkey & Cheese Stuffed Mushrooms

Servings: 5
Cooking Time: 20 Minutes
Ingredients:
- 12 ounces button mushroom caps
- 3 ounces cream cheese
- ¼ cup carrot, chopped
- 1 tsp ranch seasoning mix
- 4 tbsp hot sauce
- ¾ cup blue cheese, crumbled
- ¼ cup onion, chopped
- ½ cup turkey breasts, cooked, chopped
- Salt and black pepper, to taste
- Cooking spray

Directions:
1. Using a bowl, combine the cream cheese with the blue cheese, ranch seasoning, turkey, onion, carrot, salt, hot sauce, and pepper. Stuff each mushroom cap with this mixture, set on a lined baking sheet, spray with cooking spray, place in the oven at 425°F, and bake for 10 minutes.

Nutrition:
- Info Per Servings 8.6g Carbs, 51g Protein, 17g Fat, 486 Calories

Habanero Chicken Wings

Servings: 4
Cooking Time: 65 Minutes
Ingredients:
- 2 pounds chicken wings
- Salt and black pepper, to taste
- 3 tbsp coconut aminos
- 2 tsp white vinegar
- 3 tbsp rice vinegar
- 3 tbsp stevia
- ¼ cup chives, chopped
- ½ tsp xanthan gum
- 5 dried habanero peppers, chopped

Directions:
1. Spread the chicken wings on a lined baking sheet, sprinkle with pepper and salt, set in an oven at 370°F, and bake for 45 minutes. Put a small pan over medium heat, add in the white vinegar, coconut aminos, chives, stevia, rice vinegar, xanthan gum, and habanero peppers, bring the mixture to a boil, cook for 2 minutes, and remove from heat.
2. Dip the chicken wings into this sauce, lay them all on the baking sheet again, and bake for 10 more minutes. Serve warm.

Nutrition:
- Info Per Servings 2g Carbs, 26g Protein, 25g Fat, 416 Calories

Baked Chicken With Acorn Squash And Goat's Cheese

Servings: 6
Cooking Time: 1 Hour 15 Minutes
Ingredients:
- 6 chicken breasts, skinless and boneless
- 1 lb acorn squash, peeled and sliced
- Salt and ground black pepper, to taste
- 1 cup goat's cheese, shredded
- Cooking spray

Directions:
1. Take cooking oil and spray on a baking dish, add in chicken breasts, pepper, squash, and salt and drizzle with olive. Transfer in the oven set at 420°F, and bake for 1 hour. Scatter goat's cheese, and bake for 15 minutes. Remove to a serving plate and enjoy.

Nutrition:
- Info Per Servings 5g Carbs, 12g Protein, 16g Fat, 235 Calories

Chicken With Asparagus & Root Vegetables

Servings: 4
Cooking Time: 35 Minutes
Ingredients:
- 2 cups whipping cream
- 3 chicken breasts, boneless, skinless, chopped
- 3 tbsp butter
- ½ cup onion, chopped
- ¾ cup carrot, chopped
- 5 cups chicken stock
- Salt and black pepper, to taste
- 1 bay leaf
- 1 turnip, chopped
- 1 parsnip, chopped
- 17 ounces asparagus, trimmed
- 3 tsp fresh thyme, chopped

Directions:
1. Set a pan over medium heat and add whipping cream, allow simmering, and cook until it's reduced by half for about 7 minutes. Set another pan over medium heat and warm butter, sauté the onion for 3 minutes. Pour in the chicken stock, carrots, turnip, and parsnip, chicken, and bay leaf, bring to a boil, and simmer for 20 minutes.
2. Add in the asparagus and cook for 7 minutes. Discard the bay leaf, stir in the reduced whipping cream, adjust the seasoning and ladle the stew into serving bowls. Scatter with fresh thyme.

Nutrition:
- Info Per Servings 7.4g Carbs, 37g Protein, 31g Fat, 497 Calories

Slow-cooked Mexican Turkey Soup

Servings: 4
Cooking Time: 4 Hours 15 Minutes
Ingredients:
- 1 ½ lb turkey breasts, skinless, boneless, cubed
- 4 cups chicken stock
- 1 chopped onion
- 1 cup canned chunky salsa
- 8 ounces cheddar cheese, into chunks
- ¼ tsp cayenne red pepper
- 4 oz canned diced green chilies
- 1 tsp fresh cilantro, chopped

Directions:
1. In a slow cooker, combine the turkey with salsa, onion, green chilies, cayenne pepper, chicken stock, and cheese, and cook for 4 hours on high while covered. Open the slow cooker, sprinkle with fresh cilantro and ladle in bowls to serve.

Nutrition:
- Info Per Servings 6g Carbs, 38g Protein, 24g Fat, 387 Calories

Turkey Stew With Salsa Verde

Servings: 6
Cooking Time: 30 Minutes
Ingredients:
- 4 cups leftover turkey meat, chopped
- 2 cups green beans
- 6 cups chicken stock
- Salt and ground black pepper, to taste
- 1 tbsp canned chipotle peppers, chopped
- ½ tsp garlic powder
- ½ cup salsa verde
- 1 tsp ground coriander
- 2 tsp cumin
- ¼ cup sour cream
- 1 tbsp fresh cilantro, chopped

Directions:
1. Set a pan over medium heat. Add in the stock and heat. Stir in the green beans, and cook for 10 minutes. Place in the turkey, garlic powder, ground coriander, salt, salsa verde, chipotles, cumin, and pepper, and cook for 10 minutes.
2. Stir in the sour cream, kill the heat, and separate into bowls. Top with chopped cilantro and enjoy.

Nutrition:
- Info Per Servings 2g Carbs, 27g Protein, 11g Fat, 193 Calories

Chicken In Creamy Mushroom Sauce

Servings: 4
Cooking Time: 36 Minutes
Ingredients:
- 1 tbsp ghee
- 4 chicken breasts, cut into chunks
- Salt and black pepper to taste
- 1 packet white onion soup mix
- 2 cups chicken broth
- 15 baby bella mushrooms, sliced
- 1 cup heavy cream
- 1 small bunch parsley, chopped

Directions:
1. Melt ghee in a saucepan over medium heat, season the chicken with salt and black pepper, and brown on all sides for 6 minutes in total. Put in a plate.
2. In a bowl, stir the onion soup mix with chicken broth and add to the saucepan. Simmer for 3 minutes and add the mushrooms and chicken. Cover and simmer for another 20 minutes.
3. Stir in heavy cream and parsley, cook on low heat for 3 minutes, and season with salt and pepper.
4. Ladle the chicken with creamy sauce and mushrooms over beds of cauli mash. Garnish with parsley.

Nutrition:
- Info Per Servings 2g Carbs, 22g Protein, 38.2g Fat, 448 Calories

Lemon & Rosemary Chicken In A Skillet

Servings: 4
Cooking Time: 1 Hour And 20 Minutes
Ingredients:
- 8 chicken thighs
- 1 tsp salt
- 2 tbsp lemon juice
- 1 tsp lemon zest
- 2 tbsp olive oil
- 1 tbsp chopped rosemary
- ¼ tsp black pepper
- 1 garlic clove, minced

Directions:
1. Combine all ingredients in a bowl. Place in the fridge for one hour.
2. Heat a skillet over medium heat. Add the chicken along with the juices and cook until crispy, about 7 minutes per side.

Nutrition:
- Info Per Servings 2.5g Carbs, 31g Protein, 31g Fat, 477 Calories

Chicken Breasts With Cheddar & Pepperoni

Servings: 4
Cooking Time: 40 Minutes
Ingredients:
- 12 oz canned tomato sauce
- 1 tbsp olive oil
- 4 chicken breast halves, skinless and boneless
- Salt and ground black pepper, to taste
- 1 tsp dried oregano
- 4 oz cheddar cheese, sliced
- 1 tsp garlic powder
- 2 oz pepperoni, sliced

Directions:
1. Preheat your oven to 390°F. Using a bowl, combine chicken with oregano, salt, garlic, and pepper.
2. Heat a pan with the olive oil over medium-high heat, add in the chicken, cook each side for 2 minutes, and remove to a baking dish. Top with the cheddar cheese slices spread the sauce, then cover with pepperoni slices. Bake for 30 minutes. Serve warm garnished with fresh oregano if desired

Nutrition:
- Info Per Servings 4.5g Carbs, 32g Protein, 21g Fat, 387 Calories

Zesty Grilled Chicken

Servings: 8
Cooking Time: 35 Minutes
Ingredients:
- 2½ pounds chicken thighs and drumsticks
- 1 tbsp coconut aminos
- 1 tbsp apple cider vinegar
- A pinch of red pepper flakes
- Salt and black pepper, to taste
- ½ tsp ground ginger
- ⅓ cup butter
- 1 garlic clove, minced
- 1 tsp lime zest
- ½ cup warm water

Directions:
1. In a blender, combine the butter with water, salt, ginger, vinegar, garlic, pepper, lime zest, aminos, and pepper flakes. Pat the chicken pieces dry, lay on a pan, and top with the zesty marinade.
2. Toss to coat and refrigerate for 1 hour. Set the chicken pieces skin side down on a preheated grill over medium-high heat, cook for 10 minutes, turn, brush with some marinade, and cook for 10 minutes. Split among serving plates and enjoy.

Nutrition:
- Info Per Servings 3g Carbs, 42g Protein, 12g Fat, 375 Calories

Chicken In Creamy Tomato Sauce

Servings: 6
Cooking Time: 20 Minutes
Ingredients:
- 2 tbsp butter
- 6 chicken thighs
- Pink salt and black pepper to taste
- 14 oz canned tomato sauce
- 2 tsp Italian seasoning
- ½ cup heavy cream
- 1 cup shredded Parmesan cheese
- Parmesan cheese to garnish.

Directions:
1. In a saucepan, melt the butter over medium heat, season the chicken with salt and black pepper, and cook for 5 minutes on each side to brown. Plate the chicken.
2. Pour the tomato sauce and Italian seasoning in the pan and cook covered for 8 minutes. Adjust the taste with salt and black pepper and stir in the heavy cream and Parmesan cheese.
3. Once the cheese has melted, return the chicken to the pot, and simmer for 4 minutes, making sure to coat the chicken with the sauce while cooking.
4. Dish the chicken with sauce, garnish with more Parmesan cheese, and serve with zoodles.

Nutrition:
- Info Per Servings 2g Carbs, 24g Protein, 38.2g Fat, 456 Calories

Spinach & Ricotta Stuffed Chicken Breasts

Servings: 3
Cooking Time: 25 Minutes
Ingredients:
- 1 cup spinach, cooked and chopped
- 3 chicken breasts
- Salt and ground black pepper, to taste
- 4 ounces cream cheese, softened
- 1/2 cup ricotta cheese, crumbled
- 1 garlic clove, peeled and minced
- 1 tbsp coconut oil
- ½ cup white wine

Directions:
1. Using a bowl, combine the ricotta cheese with cream cheese, salt, garlic, pepper, and spinach. Add the chicken breasts on a working surface, cut a pocket in each, stuff them with the spinach mixture, and add more pepper and salt.
2. Set a pan over medium-high heat and warm oil, add the stuffed chicken, cook each side for 5 minutes. Put in a baking tray, drizzle with white wine and 2 tablespoons of water and then place in the oven at 420°F. Bake for 10 minutes, arrange on a serving plate and serve.

Nutrition:
- Info Per Servings 4g Carbs, 23g Protein, 12g Fat, 305 Calories

Chicken With Anchovy Tapenade

Servings: 2
Cooking Time: 30 Minutes
Ingredients:
- 1 chicken breast, cut into 4 pieces
- 2 tbsp coconut oil
- 3 garlic cloves, and crushed
- For the tapenade
- 1 cup black olives, pitted
- 1 oz anchovy fillets, rinsed
- 1 garlic clove, crushed
- Salt and ground black pepper, to taste
- 2 tbsp olive oil
- ¼ cup fresh basil, chopped
- 1 tbsp lemon juice

Directions:
1. Using a food processor, combine the olives, salt, olive oil, basil, lemon juice, anchovy fillets, and pepper, blend well. Set a pan over medium-high heat and warm coconut oil, stir in the garlic, and cook for 2 minutes.
2. Place in the chicken pieces and cook each side for 4 minutes. Split the chicken among plates and apply a topping of the anchovy tapenade.

Nutrition:
- Info Per Servings 3g Carbs, 25g Protein, 13g Fat, 155 Calories

Eggplant & Tomato Braised Chicken Thighs

Servings: 4
Cooking Time: 45 Minutes
Ingredients:
- 2 tbsp ghee
- 1 lb chicken thighs
- Pink salt and black pepper to taste
- 2 cloves garlic, minced
- 1 can whole tomatoes
- 1 eggplant, diced
- 10 fresh basil leaves, chopped + extra to garnish

Directions:
1. Melt ghee in a saucepan over medium heat, season the chicken with salt and black pepper, and fry for 4 minutes on each side until golden brown. Remove chicken onto a plate.
2. Sauté the garlic in the ghee for 2 minutes, pour in the tomatoes, and cook covered for 8 minutes.
3. Add in the eggplant and basil. Cook for 4 minutes. Season the sauce with salt and black pepper, stir and add the chicken. Coat with sauce and simmer for 3 minutes.
4. Serve chicken with sauce on a bed of squash pasta. Garnish with extra basil.

Nutrition:
- Info Per Servings 2g Carbs, 26g Protein, 39.5g Fat, 468 Calories

Yummy Chicken Queso

Servings: 4
Cooking Time: 25 Minutes
Ingredients:
- ½ teaspoon garlic salt
- 4-ounce can diced drained green chiles
- 10-ounce can mild rotel drained
- ¾ cup medium queso dip
- 4 boneless skinless boneless fresh or thawed chicken breasts
- 5 tablespoons olive oil
- 1 cup water

Directions:
1. Add all ingredients in a pot on high fire and bring it to a boil.
2. Once boiling, lower fire to a simmer and cook for 20 minutes. Stir frequently.
3. Adjust seasoning to taste.
4. Serve and enjoy.

Nutrition:
- Info Per Servings 7.2g Carbs, 56.6g Protein, 21.7g Fat, 500 Calories

Chicken Paella With Chorizo

Servings: 6
Cooking Time: 63 Minutes
Ingredients:
- 18 chicken drumsticks
- 12 oz chorizo, chopped
- 1 white onion, chopped
- 4 oz jarred piquillo peppers, finely diced
- 2 tbsp olive oil
- ½ cup chopped parsley
- 1 tsp smoked paprika
- 2 tbsp tomato puree
- ½ cup white wine
- 1 cup chicken broth
- 2 cups cauli rice
- 1 cup chopped green beans
- 1 lemon, cut in wedges
- Salt and pepper, to taste

Directions:
1. Preheat the oven to 350°F.
2. Heat the olive oil in a cast iron pan over medium heat, meanwhile season the chicken with salt and pepper, and fry in the hot oil on both sides for 10 minutes to lightly brown. After, remove onto a plate with a perforated spoon.
3. Then, add the chorizo and onion to the hot oil, and sauté for 4 minutes. Include the tomato puree, piquillo peppers, and paprika, and let simmer for 2 minutes. Add the broth, and bring the ingredients to boil for 6 minutes until slightly reduced.
4. Stir in the cauli rice, white wine, green beans, half of the parsley, and lay the chicken on top. Transfer the pan to the oven and continue cooking for 20-25 minutes. Let the paella sit to cool for 10 minutes before serving garnished with the remaining parsley and lemon wedges.

Nutrition:
- Info Per Servings 3g Carbs, 22g Protein, 28g Fat, 440 Calories

One-pot Chicken With Mushrooms And Spinach

Servings: 4
Cooking Time: 40 Minutes
Ingredients:
- 4 chicken thighs
- 2 cups mushrooms, sliced
- 1 cup spinach, chopped
- ¼ cup butter
- Salt and black pepper, to taste
- ½ tsp onion powder
- ½ tsp garlic powder
- ½ cup water
- 1 tsp Dijon mustard
- 1 tbsp fresh tarragon, chopped

Directions:
1. Set a pan over medium-high heat and warm half of the butter, place in the thighs, and sprinkle with onion powder, pepper, garlic powder, and salt. Cook each side for 3 minutes and set on a plate.
2. Place the remaining butter to the same pan and warm. Stir in mushrooms and cook for 5 minutes. Place in water and mustard, take the chicken pieces back to the pan, and cook for 15 minutes while covered. Stir in the tarragon and spinach, and cook for 5 minutes.

Nutrition:
- Info Per Servings 1g Carbs, 32g Protein, 23g Fat, 453 Calories

Creamy Stuffed Chicken With Parma Ham

Servings: 4
Cooking Time: 40 Minutes
Ingredients:
- 4 chicken breasts
- 2 tbsp olive oil
- 3 cloves garlic, minced
- 3 shallots, finely chopped
- 4 tbsp dried mixed herbs
- 8 slices Parma ham
- 8 oz cream cheese
- 2 lemons, zested
- Salt and black pepper to taste

Directions:
1. Preheat the oven to 350°F.
2. Heat the oil in a small skillet and sauté the garlic and shallots with a pinch of salt and lemon zest for 3 minutes. Turn the heat off and let it cool. After, stir the cream cheese and mixed herbs into the shallot mixture.
3. Score a pocket in each chicken breast, fill the holes with the cream cheese mixture and cover with the cut-out chicken. Wrap each breast with two Parma ham and secure the ends with a toothpick.
4. Lay the chicken parcels on a greased baking sheet and cook in the oven for 20 minutes. After cooking, remove to rest for 4 minutes before serving with a green salad and roasted tomatoes.

Nutrition:
- Info Per Servings 2g Carbs, 26g Protein, 35g Fat, 485 Calories

Lemon Chicken Bake

Servings: 6
Cooking Time: 55 Minutes
Ingredients:
- 6 skinless chicken breasts
- 1 parsnip, cut into wedges
- Salt and ground black pepper, to taste
- Juice from 2 lemons
- Zest from 2 lemons
- Lemon rinds from 2 lemons

Directions:
1. In a baking dish, add the chicken alongside pepper and salt. Sprinkle with lemon juice. Toss well to coat, place in parsnip, lemon rinds and lemon zest, set in an oven at 370°F, and bake for 45 minutes.
2. Get rid of the lemon rinds, split the chicken onto plates, sprinkle sauce from the baking dish over.

Nutrition:
- Info Per Servings 4.5g Carbs, 25g Protein, 9g Fat, 274 Calories

Pork, Beef & Lamb Recipes

Garlic Beef & Egg Frittata

Servings: 4
Cooking Time: 30 Minutes
Ingredients:
- 3 eggs, beaten
- 3 cloves of garlic, minced
- 1 onion, chopped
- ½ pound lean ground beef
- 1 stalk green onion, sliced
- 2 tablespoons olive oil
- A dash of salt
- ¼ tsp pepper

Directions:
1. Place a small cast iron pan on medium fire and heat for 2 minutes.
2. Add beef and crumble. Cook for 5 minutes.
3. Add onion and garlic, continue cooking beef until browned, around 5 minutes more. Discard any fat.
4. Season with pepper and salt.
5. Spread beef in the pan and lower fire to low.
6. Meanwhile, whisk eggs in a bowl. Pour over meat, cover, and cook for 10 minutes on low.
7. Place pan in the oven and broil on low for 3 minutes. Let it set for 5 minutes.
8. Serve and enjoy topped with green onions.

Nutrition:
- Info Per Servings 3.8g Carbs, 22.7g Protein, 20.5g Fat, 294 Calories

Chicken Broth Beef Roast

Servings: 5
Cooking Time: 2h Mins
Ingredients:
- 2 1/2 pounds boneless beef chuck roast, cut into 2-inch cubes
- 2 onions, chopped
- 2 teaspoons caraway seeds, crushed
- 4 cups chicken broth, divided
- 2 tablespoons Hungarian paprika
- 1/2 teaspoon ground thyme
- 2 tablespoons balsamic vinegar
- salt and ground black pepper to taste
- 3 cloves garlic, crushed
- 2 tablespoons olive oil

Directions:
1. Heat olive oil in a large skillet over high heat; cook and stir beef with salt and black pepper about 5 minutes per batch. Transfer to a large stockpot and reserve drippings in the skillet.
2. Stir onions and 1/2 teaspoon salt into the reserved drippings on Medium, and cook about 5 minutes. Transfer to the stockpot with beef.
3. Whisk the paprika, caraway seeds, black pepper and thyme in the skillet over medium heat and saute for 3 minutes.
4. Add 1 cup chicken broth and stir; transfer to the beef and onion mixture.
5. In the stockpot over high heat, stir 3 cups chicken broth into beef mixture. Add garlic, vinegar and 1/2 teaspoon salt, bring to a boil. Reduce heat to low and simmer 1 1/2 to 2 hours. Serve and enjoy.

Nutrition:
- Info Per Servings 13.4g Carbs, 36g Protein, 41.2g Fat, 573 Calories

Beef Cauliflower Curry

Servings: 6
Cooking Time: 26 Minutes
Ingredients:
- 1 tbsp olive oil
- 1 ½ lb ground beef
- 1 tbsp ginger-garlic paste
- 1 tsp garam masala
- 1 can whole tomatoes
- 1 head cauliflower, cut into florets
- Pink salt and chili pepper to taste
- ¼ cup water

Directions:
1. Heat oil in a saucepan over medium heat, add the beef, ginger-garlic paste and season with garam masala. Cook for 5 minutes while breaking any lumps.
2. Stir in the tomatoes and cauliflower, season with salt and chili pepper, and cook covered for 6 minutes. Add the water and bring to a boil over medium heat for 10 minutes or until the water has reduced by half. Adjust taste with salt.
3. Spoon the curry into serving bowls and serve with shirataki rice.

Nutrition:
- Info Per Servings 2g Carbs, 22g Protein, 33g Fat, 374 Calories

Mushroom Beef Stew

Servings: 5
Cooking Time: 1h 30mins
Ingredients:
- 2 pounds beef chuck roast, cut into 1/2-inch thick strips
- 1/2 medium onion, sliced or diced
- 8 ounces sliced mushrooms
- 2 cups beef broth, divided
- Salt and pepper to taste
- 1 tablespoon butter
- 2 cloves garlic, minced
- 1 tablespoon fresh chopped chives
- 1 tablespoon olive oil

Directions:
1. Heat olive oil in a large skillet over high heat. Stir in beef with salt and pepper; cook, stirring constantly, for 6-7 minutes. Remove beef from the pan and set aside.
2. Add butter, mushrooms and onions into the pan; cook and stir over medium heat.
3. Add garlic and stir for 30 seconds. Stir in 1 cup. broth and simmer 3-4 minutes.
4. Return beef to the pan. Stir in remaining broth and chives; bring to a simmer and cook on low heat for about 1 hour, covered, stirring every 20 minutes.
5. Season with salt and pepper to taste. Serve.

Nutrition:
- Info Per Servings 4.1g Carbs, 15.8g Protein, 24.5g Fat, 307 Calories

Beef And Feta Salad

Servings: 4
Cooking Time: 35 Minutes
Ingredients:
- 3 tbsp olive oil
- ½ pound beef rump steak, cut into strips
- Salt and ground black pepper, to taste
- 1 tsp cumin
- A pinch of dried thyme
- 2 garlic cloves, minced
- 4 ounces feta cheese, crumbled
- ½ cup pecans, toasted
- 2 cups spinach
- 1½ tbsp lemon juice
- ¼ cup fresh mint, chopped

Directions:
1. Season the beef with salt, 1 tbsp of olive oil, garlic, thyme, black pepper, and cumin. Place on preheated grill over medium-high heat, and cook for 10 minutes, flip once. Sprinkle the pecans on a lined baking sheet, place in the oven at 350°F, and toast for 10 minutes.
2. Remove the grilled beef to a cutting board, leave to cool, and slice into strips.
3. In a salad bowl, combine the spinach with pepper, mint, remaining olive oil, salt, lemon juice, feta cheese, and pecans, and toss well to coat. Top with the beef slices and enjoy.

Nutrition:
- Info Per Servings 3.5g Carbs, 17g Protein, 43g Fat, 434 Calories

Beef Skewers With Ranch Dressing

Servings: 4
Cooking Time: 25 Minutes
Ingredients:
- 1 lb sirloin steak, boneless, cubed
- ¼ cup ranch dressing, divided
- Chopped scallions to garnish

Directions:
1. Preheat the grill on medium heat to 400°F and thread the beef cubes on the skewers, about 4 to 5 cubes per skewer. Brush half of the ranch dressing on the skewers (all around) and place them on the grill grate to cook for 6 minutes. Turn the skewers once and cook further for 6 minutes.
2. Brush the remaining ranch dressing on the meat and cook them for 1 more minute on each side. Plate, garnish with the scallions, and serve with a mixed veggie salad, and extra ranch dressing.

Nutrition:
- Info Per Servings 3g Carbs, 21g Protein, 14g Fat, 230 Calories

Beef Zucchini Boats

Servings: 4
Cooking Time: 45 Minutes
Ingredients:
- 2 garlic cloves, minced
- 1 tsp cumin
- 1 tbsp olive oil
- 1 pound ground beef
- ½ cup onion, chopped
- 1 tsp smoked paprika
- Salt and ground black pepper, to taste
- 4 zucchinis
- ¼ cup fresh cilantro, chopped
- ½ cup Monterey Jack cheese, shredded
- 1½ cups enchilada sauce
- 1 avocado, chopped, for serving
- Green onions, chopped, for serving
- Tomatoes, chopped, for serving

Directions:
1. Set a pan over high heat and warm the oil. Add the onions, and cook for 2 minutes. Stir in the beef, and brown for 4-5 minutes. Stir in the paprika, pepper, garlic, cumin, and salt; cook for 2 minutes.
2. Slice the zucchini in half lengthwise and scoop out the seeds. Set the zucchini in a greased baking pan, stuff each with the beef, scatter enchilada sauce on top, and spread with the Monterey cheese.
3. Bake in the oven at 350°F for 20 minutes while covered. Uncover, spread with cilantro, and bake for 5 minutes. Top with tomatoes, green onions and avocado, place on serving plates and enjoy.

Nutrition:
- Info Per Servings 7.8g Carbs, 39g Protein, 33g Fat, 422 Calories

Homemade Classic Beef Burgers

Servings: 4
Cooking Time: 15 Minutes
Ingredients:
- 1 pound ground beef
- ½ tsp onion powder
- ½ tsp garlic powder
- 2 tbsp ghee
- 1 tsp Dijon mustard
- 4 low carb buns, halved
- ¼ cup mayonnaise
- 1 tsp sriracha
- 4 tbsp cabbage slaw

Directions:
1. Mix together the beef, onion, garlic powder, mustard, salt, and black pepper; create 4 burgers. Melt the ghee in a skillet and cook the burgers for about 3 minutes per side. Serve in buns topped with mayo, sriracha, and slaw.

Nutrition:
- Info Per Servings 7.9g Carbs, 39g Protein, 55g Fat, 664 Calories

Garlicky Beef Stew

Servings: 5
Cooking Time: 2h 30mins
Ingredients:
- 4 slices bacon, cut into small pieces
- 2 1/2 pounds boneless beef chuck, cut into 2-inch pieces
- 2 onions, coarsely chopped
- 2 1/2 cups chicken stock, or as needed to cover
- 4 sprigs fresh thyme
- 4 cloves garlic, minced
- 1 1/2 teaspoon salt
- 1/2 teaspoon freshly ground black pepper, or to taste

Directions:
1. In a skillet over medium-high heat, cook bacon for 3 to 4 minutes. Turn off heat and transfer bacon into a stew pot.
2. Season beef chuck cubes with 1 teaspoon salt and black pepper to taste. Then broil beef pieces for 5 minutes on High.
3. Add beef in stew pot with bacon. Lower the heat to medium; cook and stir onions for 5 to 8 minutes; season with a large pinch of salt. Mix in the garlic, saute for 1 minute; stir in tomato paste, thyme sprigs, 1/2 teaspoon black pepper, and enough chicken broth in a skillet. Reduce heat to low and cover. Simmer stew about 2 hours.
4. Remove cover and bring stew to a boil on Medium and cook for 15 to 20 minutes.
5. Remove and discard thyme sprigs and sprinkle salt and pepper to taste.

Nutrition:
- Info Per Servings 11.3g Carbs, 29.4g Protein, 24.6g Fat, 528 Calories

Creamy Pork Chops

Servings: 3
Cooking Time: 50 Minutes
Ingredients:
- 8 ounces mushrooms, sliced
- 1 tsp garlic powder
- 1 onion, peeled and chopped
- 1 cup heavy cream
- 3 pork chops, boneless
- 1 tsp ground nutmeg
- ¼ cup coconut oil

Directions:
1. Set a pan over medium heat and warm the oil, add in the onions and mushrooms, and cook for 4 minutes. Stir in the pork chops, season with garlic powder, and nutmeg, and sear until browned.
2. Put the pan in the oven at 350°F, and bake for 30 minutes. Remove pork chops to bowls and maintain warm. Place the pan over medium heat, pour in the heavy cream and vinegar over the mushrooms mixture, and cook for 5 minutes; remove from heat. Sprinkle sauce over pork chops and enjoy.

Nutrition:
- Info Per Servings 6.8g Carbs, 42g Protein, 40g Fat, 612 Calories

Beef Stew With Bacon

Servings: 6
Cooking Time: 1 Hour 15 Minutes
Ingredients:
- 8 ounces bacon, chopped
- 4 lb beef meat for stew, cubed
- 4 garlic cloves, minced
- 2 brown onions, chopped
- 2 tbsp olive oil
- 4 tbsp red vinegar
- 4 cups beef stock
- 2 tbsp tomato puree
- 2 cinnamon sticks
- 3 lemon peel strips
- ½ cup fresh parsley, chopped
- 4 thyme sprigs
- 2 tbsp butter
- Salt and black pepper, to taste

Directions:
1. Set a saucepan over medium-high heat and warm oil, add in the garlic, bacon, and onion, and cook for 5 minutes. Stir in the beef, and cook until slightly brown. Pour in the vinegar, pepper, butter, lemon peel strips, stock, salt, tomato puree, cinnamon sticks and thyme; stir for 3 minutes.
2. Cook for 1 hour while covered. Get rid of the thyme, lemon peel, and cinnamon sticks. Split into serving bowls and sprinkle with parsley to serve.

Nutrition:
- Info Per Servings 5.7g Carbs, 63g Protein, 36g Fat, 592 Calories

Classic Meatloaf

Servings: 3
Cooking Time: 40 Mins
Directions:
1. Preheat the oven to 325 degrees F.
2. Place the celery, onion and garlic in a food processor.
3. Place the minced vegetables into a large mixing bowl, and mix in ground chuck, Italian herbs, salt, black pepper, and cayenne pepper.
4. Whisk in the almond flour, stirring well, about 1 minute.
5. Sprinkle the olive oil into a baking dish and place meat into the dish. Shape the ball into a loaf. Bake in the preheated oven for 15 minutes.
6. In a small bowl, mix together ketchup, Dijon mustard, and hot sauce, stirring well to combined.
7. Bake the meatloaf for 30 to 40 more minutes at least 160 degrees F.

Nutrition:
- Info Per Servings 10.8g Carbs, 21.6g Protein, 19g Fat, 300 Calories

Pork Osso Bucco

Servings: 6
Cooking Time: 1 Hour 55 Minutes
Ingredients:
- 4 tbsp butter, softened
- 6 pork shanks
- 2 tbsp olive oil
- 3 cloves garlic, minced
- 1 cup diced tomatoes
- Salt and black pepper to taste
- ½ cup chopped onions
- ½ cup chopped celery
- ½ cup chopped carrots
- 2 cups Cabernet Sauvignon
- 5 cups beef broth
- ½ cup chopped parsley + extra to garnish
- 2 tsp lemon zest

Directions:
1. Melt the butter in a large saucepan over medium heat. Season the pork with salt and pepper and brown it for 12 minutes; remove to a plate.
2. In the same pan, sauté 2 cloves of garlic and onions in the oil, for 3 minutes then return the pork shanks. Stir in the Cabernet, carrots, celery, tomatoes, and beef broth with a season of salt and pepper. Cover the pan and let it simmer on low heat for 1 ½ hours basting the pork every 15 minutes with the sauce.
3. In a bowl, mix the remaining garlic, parsley, and lemon zest to make a gremolata, and stir the mixture into the sauce when it is ready. Turn the heat off and dish the Osso Bucco. Garnish with parsley and serve with a creamy turnip mash.

Nutrition:
- Info Per Servings 6.1g Carbs, 34g Protein, 40g Fat, 590 Calories

Pancetta Sausage With Kale

Servings: 10
Cooking Time: 25 Minutes
Ingredients:
- ½ gallon chicken broth
- A drizzle of olive oil
- 1 cup heavy cream
- 2 cups kale
- 6 pancetta slices, chopped
- 1 pound radishes, chopped
- 2 garlic cloves, minced
- Salt and black pepper, to taste
- A pinch of red pepper flakes
- 1 onion, chopped
- 1½ pounds hot pork sausage, chopped

Directions:
1. Set a pot over medium heat. Add in a drizzle of olive oil and warm. Stir in garlic, onion, pancetta, and sausage; cook for 5 minutes. Pour in broth, radishes, and kale, and simmer for 10 minutes.
2. Stir in the, salt, red pepper flakes, pepper, and heavy cream, and cook for about 5 minutes. Split among serving bowls and enjoy the meal.

Nutrition:
- Info Per Servings 5.4g Carbs, 21g Protein, 29g Fat, 386 Calories

Sweet Chipotle Grilled Ribs

Servings: 4
Cooking Time: 32 Minutes
Ingredients:
- 2 tbsp erythritol
- Pink salt and black pepper to taste
- 1 tbsp olive oil
- 3 tsp chipotle powder
- 1 tsp garlic powder
- 1 lb spare ribs
- 4 tbsp sugar-free BBQ sauce + extra for serving

Directions:
1. Mix the erythritol, salt, pepper, oil, chipotle, and garlic powder. Brush on the meaty sides of the ribs and wrap in foil. Sit for 30 minutes to marinate.
2. Preheat oven to 400°F, place wrapped ribs on a baking sheet, and cook for 40 minutes to be cooked through. Remove ribs and aluminium foil, brush with BBQ sauce, and brown under the broiler for 10 minutes on both sides. Slice and serve with extra BBQ sauce and lettuce tomato salad.

Nutrition:
- Info Per Servings 3g Carbs, 21g Protein, 33g Fat, 395 Calories

Cocoa-crusted Pork Tenderloin

Servings: 2
Cooking Time: 25 Minutes
Ingredients:
- 1-pound pork tenderloin, trimmed from fat
- 1 tablespoon cocoa powder
- 1 teaspoon instant coffee powder
- ½ teaspoon ground cinnamon
- ½ teaspoon chili powder
- 1 tablespoon olive oil
- Pepper and salt to taste

Directions:
1. In a bowl, dust the pork tenderloin with cocoa powder, coffee, cinnamon, pepper, salt, and chili powder.
2. In a skillet, heat the oil and sear the meat for 5 minutes on both sides over low to medium flame.
3. Transfer the pork in a baking dish and cook in the oven for 15 minutes in a 350F preheated oven.

Nutrition:
- Info Per Servings 2.0g Carbs, 60.0g Protein, 15.0g Fat, 395 Calories

North African Lamb

Servings: 4
Cooking Time: 25 Minutes
Ingredients:
- 2 tsp paprika
- 2 garlic cloves, minced
- 2 tsp dried oregano
- 2 tbsp sumac
- 12 lamb cutlets
- ¼ cup sesame oil
- 2 tbsp water
- 2 tsp cumin
- 4 carrots, sliced
- ¼ cup fresh parsley, chopped
- 2 tsp harissa paste
- 1 tbsp red wine vinegar
- Salt and black pepper, to taste
- 2 tbsp black olives, sliced
- 2 cucumbers, sliced thin

Directions:
1. Using a bowl, combine the cutlets with the paprika, oregano, pepper, water, half of the oil, sumac, garlic, and salt, and rub well. Add the carrots in a pot, cover with the water, bring to a boil over medium-high heat, cook for 2 minutes then drain before placing them in a salad bowl.
2. Place the cucumbers and olives to the carrots. In another bowl, combine the harissa with the rest of the oil, a splash of water, parsley, vinegar, and cumin. Place this to the carrots mixture, season with pepper and salt, and toss well to coat. Heat a grill over medium heat and arrange the lamb cutlets on it, grill each side for 3 minutes, and split among separate plates. Serve alongside the carrot salad.

Nutrition:
- Info Per Servings 4g Carbs, 34g Protein, 32g Fat, 445 Calories

Beef Sausage Casserole

Servings: 8
Cooking Time: 60 Minutes
Ingredients:
- ⅓ cup almond flour
- 2 eggs
- 2 pounds beef sausage, chopped
- Salt and black pepper, to taste
- 1 tbsp dried parsley
- ¼ tsp red pepper flakes
- ¼ cup Parmesan cheese, grated
- ¼ tsp onion powder
- ½ tsp garlic powder
- ¼ tsp dried oregano
- 1 cup ricotta cheese
- 1 cup sugar-free marinara sauce
- 1½ cups cheddar cheese, shredded

Directions:
1. Using a bowl, combine the sausage, pepper, pepper flakes, oregano, eggs, Parmesan cheese, onion powder, almond flour, salt, parsley, and garlic powder. Form balls, lay them on a lined baking sheet, place in the oven at 370°F, and bake for 15 minutes.
2. Remove the balls from the oven and cover with half of the marinara sauce. Pour ricotta cheese all over followed by the rest of the marinara sauce. Scatter the cheddar cheese and bake in the oven for 10 minutes. Allow the meatballs casserole to cool before serving.

Nutrition:
- Info Per Servings 4g Carbs, 32g Protein, 35g Fat, 456 Calories

Italian Shredded Beef

Servings: 6
Cooking Time: 42 Minutes
Ingredients:
- 3 pounds chuck roast, trimmed from excess fat and cut into chunks
- 1 packet Italian salad dressing mix
- 8 ounces pepperoncini pepper slices
- 1 can beef broth
- Salt and pepper to taste
- 1 cup water
- 1 tsp oil

Directions:
1. Place a heavy-bottomed pot on medium-high fire and heat for 2 minutes. Add oil and swirl to coat the bottom and sides of pot and heat for a minute.
2. Season roast with pepper and salt. Brown roast for 4 minutes per side. Transfer to a chopping board and chop into 4 equal pieces.
3. Add remaining ingredients to the pot along with sliced beef.
4. Cover and simmer for 30 minutes or until beef is fork-tender. Stir the bottom of the pot now and then. Turn off the fire.
5. With two forks, shred beef.
6. Turn on fire to high and boil uncovered until sauce is rendered, around 5 minutes.

Nutrition:
- Info Per Servings 6.6g Carbs, 61.5g Protein, 20.5g Fat, 455 Calories

Spicy Mesquite Ribs

Servings: 6
Cooking Time: 8 Hours 45 Minutes
Ingredients:
- 3 racks pork ribs, silver lining removed
- 2 cups sugar-free BBQ sauce
- 2 tbsp erythritol
- 2 tsp chili powder
- 2 tsp cumin powder
- 2 tsp onion powder
- 2 tsp smoked paprika
- 2 tsp garlic powder
- Salt and black pepper to taste
- 1 tsp mustard powder

Directions:
1. Preheat a smoker to 400°F using mesquite wood to create flavor in the smoker.
2. In a bowl, mix the erythritol, chili powder, cumin powder, black pepper, onion powder, smoked paprika, garlic powder, salt, and mustard powder. Rub the ribs and let marinate for 30 minutes.
3. Place on the grill grate, and cook at reduced heat of 225°F for 4 hours. Flip the ribs after and continue cooking for 4 hours. Brush the ribs with bbq sauce on both sides and sear them in increased heat for 3 minutes per side. Remove the ribs and let sit for 4 minutes before slicing. Serve with red cabbage coleslaw.

Nutrition:
- Info Per Servings 0g Carbs, 44.5g Protein, 36.6g Fat, 580 Calories

Grilled Flank Steak With Lime Vinaigrette

Servings: 6
Cooking Time: 10 Minutes
Ingredients:
- 2 tablespoons lime juice, freshly squeezed
- ¼ cup chopped fresh cilantro
- 1 tablespoon ground cumin
- ¼ teaspoon red pepper flakes
- ¾ pound flank steak
- 2 tablespoons extra virgin olive oil
- ½ teaspoon ground black pepper
- ¼ tsp salt

Directions:
1. Heat the grill to low, medium heat
2. In a food processor, place all ingredients except for the cumin, red pepper flakes, and flank steak. Pulse until smooth. This will be the vinaigrette sauce. Set aside.
3. Season the flank steak with ground cumin and red pepper flakes and allow to marinate for at least 10 minutes.
4. Place the steak on the grill rack and cook for 5 minutes on each side. Cut into the center to check the doneness of the meat. You can also insert a meat thermometer to check the internal temperature.
5. Remove from the grill and allow to stand for 5 minutes.
6. Slice the steak to 2 inches long and toss the vinaigrette to flavor the meat.
7. Serve with salad if desired.

Nutrition:
- Info Per Servings 1.0g Carbs, 13.0g Protein, 1.0g Fat, 65 Calories

Spanish Frittata

Servings: 6
Cooking Time: 26 Minutes
Ingredients:
- 3 large eggs, beaten
- ½ chorizo sausage, sliced
- ½ zucchini, sliced
- A dash of oregano
- A dash of Spanish paprika
- Pepper and salt to taste
- 3 tablespoons olive oil

Directions:
1. Preheat the air fryer for 5 minutes.
2. Combine all ingredients in a mixing bowl until well-incorporated.
3. Pour into a greased baking dish that will fit in the air fryer basket.
4. Place the baking dish in the air fryer.
5. Close and cook for 15 minutes at 350F.

Nutrition:
- Info Per Servings 0.5g Carbs, 1.8g Protein, 9.4g Fat, 93 Calories

Beef Meatballs With Onion Sauce

Servings: 5
Cooking Time: 35 Minutes
Ingredients:
- 2 pounds ground beef
- Salt and black pepper, to taste
- ½ tsp garlic powder
- 1 ¼ tbsp coconut aminos
- 1 cup beef stock
- ¾ cup almond flour
- 1 tbsp fresh parsley, chopped
- 1 tbsp dried onion flakes
- 1 onion, sliced
- 2 tbsp butter
- ¼ cup sour cream

Directions:
1. Using a bowl, combine the beef with salt, garlic powder, almond flour, onion flakes, parsley, 1 tablespoon coconut aminos, black pepper, ¼ cup of beef stock. Form 6 patties, place them on a baking sheet, put in the oven at 370°F, and bake for 18 minutes.
2. Set a pan with the butter over medium heat, stir in the onion, and cook for 3 minutes. Stir in the remaining beef stock, sour cream, and remaining coconut aminos, and bring to a simmer.
3. Remove from heat, adjust the seasoning with black pepper and salt. Serve the meatballs topped with onion sauce.

Nutrition:
- Info Per Servings 6g Carbs, 32g Protein, 23g Fat, 435 Calories

Rack Of Lamb In Red Bell Pepper Butter Sauce

Servings: 4
Cooking Time: 65 Minutes + Cooling Time
Ingredients:
- 1 lb rack of lamb
- Salt to cure
- 3 cloves garlic, minced
- ⅓ cup olive oil
- ⅓ cup white wine
- 6 sprigs fresh rosemary
- Water for soaking
- Sauce
- 2 tbsp olive oil
- 1 large red bell pepper, seeded, diced
- 2 cloves garlic, minced
- 1 cup chicken broth
- 2 oz butter
- Salt and white pepper to taste

Directions:
1. Fill a large bowl with water and soak in the lamb for 30 minutes. Drain the meat after and season with salt. Let the lamb sit on a rack to drain completely and then rinse it afterward. Put in a bowl.
2. Mix the olive oil with wine and garlic, and brush the mixture all over the lamb. Drop the rosemary sprigs on it, cover the bowl with plastic wrap, and place in the refrigerator to marinate the meat.
3. The next day, preheat the grill to 450°F and cook the lamb for 6 minutes on both sides. Remove after and let rest for 4 minutes.
4. Heat the olive oil in a frying pan and sauté the garlic and bell pepper for 5 minutes. Pour in the chicken broth and continue cooking the ingredients until the liquid reduces by half, about 10 minutes. Add the butter, salt, and pepper. Stir to melt the butter and turn the heat off.
5. Use the stick blender to puree the ingredients until very smooth and strain the sauce through a fine mesh into a bowl. Slice the lamb, serve with the sauce, and your favorite red wine.

Nutrition:
- Info Per Servings 2g Carbs, 46g Protein, 25g Fat, 415 Calories

Beef Steak Filipino Style

Servings: 6
Cooking Time: 25 Minutes
Ingredients:
- 2 tablespoons coconut oil
- 1 onion, sliced
- 4 beef steaks
- 2 tablespoons lemon juice, freshly squeezed
- ¼ cup coconut aminos
- 1 tsp salt
- Pepper to taste

Directions:
1. In a nonstick fry pan, heat oil on medium-high fire.
2. Pan-fry beef steaks and season with coconut aminos.
3. Cook until dark brown, around 7 minutes per side. Transfer to a plate.
4. Sauté onions in the same pan until caramelized, around 8 minutes. Season with lemon juice and return steaks in the pan. Mix well.
5. Serve and enjoy.

Nutrition:
- Info Per Servings 0.7g Carbs, 25.3g Protein, 27.1g Fat, 347 Calories

Russian Beef Gratin

Servings: 5
Cooking Time: 45 Minutes
Ingredients:
- 2 tsp onion flakes
- 2 pounds ground beef
- 2 garlic cloves, minced
- Salt and ground black pepper, to taste
- 1 cup mozzarella cheese, shredded
- 2 cups fontina cheese, shredded
- 1 cup Russian dressing
- 2 tbsp sesame seeds, toasted
- 20 dill pickle slices
- 1 iceberg lettuce head, torn

Directions:
1. Set a pan over medium heat, place in the beef, garlic, salt, onion flakes, and pepper, and cook for 5 minutes. Remove and set to a baking dish, stir in half of the Russian dressing, mozzarella cheese, and spread 1 cup of the fontina cheese.
2. Lay the pickle slices on top, spread over the remaining fontina cheese and sesame seeds, place in the oven at 350°F, and bake for 20 minutes. Split the lettuce on serving plates, apply a topping of beef gratin, and the remaining Russian dressing.

Nutrition:
- Info Per Servings 5g Carbs, 41g Protein, 48g Fat, 584 Calories

Beef Mushroom Meatloaf

Servings: 12
Cooking Time: 1 Hour And 15 Minutes
Ingredients:
- 3 pounds ground beef
- ½ cup chopped onions
- ½ cup almond flour
- 2 garlic cloves, minced
- 1 cup sliced mushrooms
- 3 eggs
- ¼ tsp pepper
- 2 tbsp chopped parsley
- ¼ cup chopped bell peppers
- ⅓ cup grated Parmesan cheese
- 1 tsp balsamic vinegar
- 1 tsp salt
- Glaze:
- 2 cups balsamic vinegar
- 1 tbsp sweetener
- 2 tbsp sugar-free ketchup

Directions:
1. Combine all meatloaf ingredients in a large bowl. Press this mixture into 2 greased loaf pans. Bake at 370°F for about 30 minutes.
2. Meanwhile, make the glaze by combining all ingredients in a saucepan over medium heat. Simmer for 20 minutes, until the glaze is thickened. Pour ¼ cup of the glaze over the meatloaf. Save the extra for future use. Put the meatloaf back in the oven and cook for 20 more minutes.

Nutrition:
- Info Per Servings 6g Carbs, 23g Protein, 19g Fat, 294 Calories

Beef Cheeseburger Casserole

Servings: 6
Cooking Time: 30 Minutes
Ingredients:
- 2 lb ground beef
- Pink salt and black pepper to taste
- 1 cup cauli rice
- 2 cups chopped cabbage
- 14 oz can diced tomatoes
- ¼ cup water
- 1 cup shredded colby jack cheese

Directions:
1. Preheat oven to 370°F and grease a baking dish with cooking spray. Put beef in a pot and season with salt and black pepper and cook over medium heat for 6 minutes until no longer pink. Drain the grease. Add cauli rice, cabbage, tomatoes, and water. Stir and bring to boil covered for 5 minutes to thicken the sauce. Adjust taste with salt and black pepper.
2. Spoon the beef mixture into the baking dish and spread evenly. Sprinkle with cheese and bake in the oven for 15 minutes until cheese has melted and it's golden brown. Remove and cool for 4 minutes and serve with low carb crusted bread.

Nutrition:
- Info Per Servings 5g Carbs, 20g Protein, 25g Fat, 385 Calories

One Pot Tomato Pork Chops Stew

Servings: 6
Cooking Time: 30 Minutes
Ingredients:
- 6 pork chops
- 1 onion, chopped
- 1 bay leaf
- ½ cup tomato paste
- 1 tsp oil
- Salt and pepper to taste
- 1/2 cup water

Directions:
1. Place a heavy-bottomed pot on medium-high fire and heat for 2 minutes. Add oil and heat for a minute more.
2. Add pork chops and sear for 3 minutes per side. Transfer to a chopping board and slice into bite-sized pieces.
3. In the same pot, sauté onion, bay leaf, and tomato paste for a minute. Add water and deglaze the pot.
4. Return chops to the pot, season with pepper and salt.
5. Cover and simmer for 20 minutes.

Nutrition:
- Info Per Servings 6.5g Carbs, 41.5g Protein, 17.5g Fat, 357 Calories

Moroccan Beef Stew

Servings: 4
Cooking Time: 40 Minutes
Ingredients:
- 1 medium onion, chopped coarsely
- 2-lbs London broil roast, chopped into 2-inch cubes
- ¼ cup prunes
- 1 ¼ teaspoons curry powder
- ½ teaspoon ground cinnamon
- ½ teaspoon salt
- 2 cups water

Directions:
1. Add all ingredients in a pot on high fire and bring to a boil.
2. Once boiling, lower fire to a simmer and cook for 35 minutes.
3. Adjust seasoning to taste.
4. Serve and enjoy.

Nutrition:
- Info Per Servings 8.3g Carbs, 40.6g Protein, 49.6g Fat, 658 Calories

Meatballs With Ranch-buffalo Sauce

Servings: 10
Cooking Time: 30 Minutes
Ingredients:
- 1 packet Ranch dressing dry mix
- 1 bottle red-hot wings buffalo sauce
- 1 bag frozen Rosina Italian Style Meatballs
- 5 tablespoons butter
- 1 cup water
- Pepper and salt to taste

Directions:
1. Add all ingredients in a pot on high fire and bring to a boil.
2. Once boiling, lower fire to a simmer and cook for 25 minutes.
3. Adjust seasoning to taste.
4. Serve and enjoy.

Nutrition:
- Info Per Servings 1.2g Carbs, 36.0g Protein, 27.9g Fat, 400 Calories

Soups, Stew & Salads Recipes

Grilled Steak Salad With Pickled Peppers

Servings: 4
Cooking Time: 15 Minutes
Ingredients:
- 1 lb skirt steak, sliced
- Salt and black pepper to season
- 1 tsp olive oil
- 1 ½ cups mixed salad greens
- 3 chopped pickled peppers
- 2 tbsp red wine vinaigrette
- ½ cup crumbled queso fresco

Directions:
1. Brush the steak slices with olive oil and season with salt and pepper on both sides.
2. Heat frying pan over high heat and cook the steaks on each side to the desired doneness, for about 5-6 minutes. Remove to a bowl, cover and leave to rest while you make the salad.
3. Mix the salad greens, pickled peppers, and vinaigrette in a salad bowl. Add the beef and sprinkle with cheese. Serve the salad with roasted parsnips.

Nutrition:
- Info Per Servings 2g Carbs, 18g Protein, 26g Fat, 315 Calories

Beef Reuben Soup

Servings: 6
Cooking Time: 20 Minutes
Ingredients:
- 1 onion, diced
- 6 cups beef stock
- 1 tsp caraway seeds
- 2 celery stalks, diced
- 2 garlic cloves, minced
- 2 cups heavy cream
- 1 cup sauerkraut
- 1 pound corned beef, chopped
- 3 tbsp butter
- 1 ½ cup swiss cheese
- Salt and black pepper, to taste

Directions:
1. Melt the butter in a large pot. Add onion and celery, and fry for 3 minutes until tender. Add garlic and cook for another minute.
2. Pour the beef stock over and stir in sauerkraut, salt, caraway seeds, and add a pinch of pepper. Bring to a boil. Reduce the heat to low, and add the corned beef. Cook for about 15 minutes, adjust the seasoning. Stir in heavy cream and cheese and cook for 1 minute.

Nutrition:
- Info Per Servings 8g Carbs, 23g Protein, 37g Fat, 450 Calories

Chicken Creamy Soup

Servings: 4
Cooking Time: 15 Minutes
Ingredients:
- 2 cups cooked and shredded chicken
- 3 tbsp butter, melted
- 4 cups chicken broth
- 4 tbsp chopped cilantro
- ⅓ cup buffalo sauce
- ½ cup cream cheese
- Salt and black pepper, to taste

Directions:
1. Blend the butter, buffalo sauce, and cream cheese, in a food processor, until smooth. Transfer to a pot, add the chicken broth and heat until hot but do not bring to a boil. Stir in chicken, salt, black pepper and cook until heated through. When ready, remove to soup bowls and serve garnished with cilantro.

Nutrition:
- Info Per Servings 5g Carbs, 26.5g Protein, 29.5g Fat, 406 Calories

Caesar Salad With Smoked Salmon And Poached Eggs

Servings: 4
Cooking Time: 15 Minutes
Ingredients:
- 3 cups water
- 8 eggs
- 2 cups torn romaine lettuce
- ½ cup smoked salmon, chopped
- 6 slices bacon
- 2 tbsp Heinz low carb Caesar dressing

Directions:
1. Boil the water in a pot over medium heat for 5 minutes and bring to simmer. Crack each egg into a small bowl and gently slide into the water. Poach for 2 to 3 minutes, remove with a perforated spoon, transfer to a paper towel to dry, and plate. Poach the remaining 7 eggs.
2. Put the bacon in a skillet and fry over medium heat until browned and crispy, about 6 minutes, turning once. Remove, allow cooling, and chop in small pieces.
3. Toss the lettuce, smoked salmon, bacon, and caesar dressing in a salad bowl. Divide the salad into 4 plates, top with two eggs each, and serve immediately or chilled.

Nutrition:
- Info Per Servings 5g Carbs, 8g Protein, 21g Fat, 260 Calories

Balsamic Cucumber Salad

Servings: 6
Cooking Time: 0 Minutes
Ingredients:
- 1 large English cucumber, halved and sliced
- 1 cup grape tomatoes, halved
- 1 medium red onion, sliced thinly
- ¼ cup balsamic vinaigrette
- ¾ cup feta cheese
- Salt and pepper to taste
- ¼ cup olive oil

Directions:
1. Place all ingredients in a bowl.
2. Toss to coat everything with the dressing.
3. Allow chilling before serving.

Nutrition:
- Info Per Servings 9g Carbs, 4.8g Protein, 16.7g Fat, 253 Calories

Slow Cooker Beer Soup With Cheddar & Sausage

Servings: 8
Cooking Time: 8 Hr
Ingredients:
- 1 cup heavy cream
- 10 ounces sausages, sliced
- 1 cup celery, chopped
- 1 cup carrots, chopped
- 4 garlic cloves, minced
- 8 ounces cream cheese
- 1 tsp red pepper flakes
- 6 ounces beer
- 16 ounces beef stock
- 1 onion, diced
- 1 cup cheddar cheese, grated
- Salt and black pepper, to taste
- Fresh cilantro, chopped, to garnish

Directions:
1. Turn on the slow cooker. Add beef stock, beer, sausages, carrots, onion, garlic, celery, salt, red pepper flakes, and black pepper, and stir to combine. Pour in enough water to cover all the ingredients by roughly 2 inches. Close the lid and cook for 6 hours on Low.
2. Open the lid and stir in the heavy cream, cheddar, and cream cheese, and cook for 2 more hours. Ladle the soup into bowls and garnish with cilantro before serving. Yummy!

Nutrition:
- Info Per Servings 4g Carbs, 5g Protein, 17g Fat, 244 Calories

Cream Of Thyme Tomato Soup

Servings: 6
Cooking Time: 20 Minutes

Ingredients:
- 2 tbsp ghee
- 2 large red onions, diced
- ½ cup raw cashew nuts, diced
- 2 cans tomatoes
- 1 tsp fresh thyme leaves + extra to garnish
- 1 ½ cups water
- Salt and black pepper to taste
- 1 cup heavy cream

Directions:
1. Melt ghee in a pot over medium heat and sauté the onions for 4 minutes until softened.
2. Stir in the tomatoes, thyme, water, cashews, and season with salt and black pepper. Cover and bring to simmer for 10 minutes until thoroughly cooked.
3. Open, turn the heat off, and puree the ingredients with an immersion blender. Adjust to taste and stir in the heavy cream. Spoon into soup bowls and serve with low carb parmesan cheese toasts.

Nutrition:
- Info Per Servings 3g Carbs, 11g Protein, 27g Fat, 310 Calories

Spicy Chicken Bean Soup

Servings: 8
Cooking Time: 1h 20 Mins

Ingredients:
- 8 skinless, boneless chicken breast halves
- 5 cubes chicken bouillon
- 2 cans peeled and diced tomatoes
- 1 container sour cream
- 1 cups frozen cut green beans
- 3 tablespoons. olive oil
- Salt and black pepper to taste
- 1 onion, chopped
- 3 cloves garlic, chopped
- 1 cups frozen cut green beans

Directions:
1. Heat olive oil in a large pot over medium heat, add onion, garlic and cook until tender. Stir in water, chicken, salt, pepper, bouillon cubes and bring to boil, simmer for 1 hour on Low. Remove chicken from the pot, reserve 5 cups broth and slice.
2. Stir in the remaining ingredients in the pot and simmer 30 minutes. Serve and enjoy.

Nutrition:
- Info Per Servings 7.6g Carbs, 26.5g Protein, 15.3g Fat, 275.1 Calories

Citrusy Brussels Sprouts Salad

Servings: 6
Cooking Time: 3 Minutes
Ingredients:
- 2 tablespoons olive oil
- ¾ pound Brussels sprouts
- 1 cup walnuts
- Juice from 1 lemon
- ½ cup grated parmesan cheese
- Salt and pepper to taste

Directions:
1. Heat oil in a skillet over medium flame and sauté the Brussels sprouts for 3 minutes until slightly wilted. Removed from heat and allow to cool.
2. In a bowl, toss together the cooled Brussels sprouts and the rest of the ingredients.
3. Toss to coat.

Nutrition:
- Info Per Servings 8g Carbs, 6g Protein, 23g Fat, 259 Calories

Simplified French Onion Soup

Servings: 5
Cooking Time: 30 Minutes
Ingredients:
- 3 large onions, sliced
- 2 bay leaves
- 5 cups Beef Bone Broth
- 1 teaspoon dried thyme
- 1-oz Gruyere cheese, sliced into 5 equal pieces
- Pepper to taste
- 4 tablespoons oil

Directions:
1. Place a heavy-bottomed pot on medium-high fire and heat pot for 3 minutes.
2. Add oil and heat for 2 minutes. Stir in onions and sauté for 5 minutes.
3. Lower fire to medium-low, continue sautéing onions for 10 minutes until soft and browned, but not burned.
4. Add remaining ingredients and mix well.
5. Bring to a boil, lower fire to a simmer, cover and cook for 5 minutes.
6. Ladle into bowls, top with cheese.
7. Let it sit for 5 minutes.
8. Serve and enjoy.

Nutrition:
- Info Per Servings 9.9g Carbs, 4.3g Protein, 16.8g Fat, 208 Calories

Green Minestrone Soup

Servings: 4
Cooking Time: 25 Minutes
Ingredients:
- 2 tbsp ghee
- 2 tbsp onion garlic puree
- 2 heads broccoli, cut in florets
- 2 stalks celery, chopped
- 5 cups vegetable broth
- 1 cup baby spinach
- Salt and black pepper to taste

Directions:
1. Melt the ghee in a saucepan over medium heat and sauté the garlic for 3 minutes until softened. Mix in the broccoli and celery, and cook for 4 minutes until slightly tender. Pour in the broth, bring to a boil, then reduce the heat to medium-low and simmer covered for about 5 minutes.
2. Drop in the spinach to wilt, adjust the seasonings, and cook for 4 minutes. Ladle soup into serving bowls. Serve with a sprinkle of grated Gruyere cheese and freshly baked low carb carrot bread.

Nutrition:
- Info Per Servings 2g Carbs, 8g Protein, 20.3g Fat, 227 Calories

Creamy Cauliflower Soup With Bacon Chips

Servings: 4
Cooking Time: 25 Minutes
Ingredients:
- 2 tbsp ghee
- 1 onion, chopped
- 2 head cauliflower, cut into florets
- 2 cups water
- Salt and black pepper to taste
- 3 cups almond milk
- 1 cup shredded white cheddar cheese
- 3 bacon strips

Directions:
1. Melt the ghee in a saucepan over medium heat and sauté the onion for 3 minutes until fragrant.
2. Include the cauli florets, sauté for 3 minutes to slightly soften, add the water, and season with salt and black pepper. Bring to a boil, and then reduce the heat to low. Cover and cook for 10 minutes.
3. Puree cauliflower with an immersion blender until the ingredients are evenly combined and stir in the almond milk and cheese until the cheese melts. Adjust taste with salt and black pepper.
4. In a non-stick skillet over high heat, fry the bacon, until crispy. Divide soup between serving bowls, top with crispy bacon, and serve hot.

Nutrition:
- Info Per Servings 6g Carbs, 8g Protein, 37g Fat, 402 Calories

Butternut And Kale Soup

Servings: 10
Cooking Time: 30 Minutes
Ingredients:
- 1 package Italian turkey sausage links, casings removed
- ½ medium butternut squash, peeled and cubed
- 2 cartons reduced-sodium chicken broth
- 1 bunch kale, trimmed and coarsely chopped
- 1/2 cup shaved Parmesan cheese
- 6 tablespoons butter
- Water
- Salt to taste

Directions:
1. In a stockpot, cook sausage over medium heat until no longer pink, breaking into crumbles, 8-10 minutes.
2. Add squash and broth; bring to a boil. Gradually stir in kale, allowing it to wilt slightly between additions. Return to a boil.
3. Reduce heat; simmer, uncovered, until vegetables are tender, 15-20 minutes. Top servings with cheese.

Nutrition:
- Info Per Servings 5.3g Carbs, 13g Protein, 5g Fat, 118 Calories

Warm Baby Artichoke Salad

Servings: 4
Cooking Time: 30 Minutes
Ingredients:
- 6 baby artichokes
- 6 cups water
- 1 tbsp lemon juice
- ¼ cup cherry peppers, halved
- ¼ cup pitted olives, sliced
- ¼ cup olive oil
- ¼ tsp lemon zest
- 2 tsp balsamic vinegar, sugar-free
- 1 tbsp chopped dill
- ½ tsp salt
- ¼ tsp black pepper
- 1 tbsp capers
- ¼ tsp caper brine

Directions:
1. Combine the water and salt in a pot over medium heat. Trim and halve the artichokes; add to the pot. Bring to a boil, lower the heat, and let simmer for 20 minutes until tender.
2. Combine the rest of the ingredients, except the olives in a bowl. Drain and place the artichokes in a serving plate. Pour the prepared mixture over; toss to combine well. Serve topped with the olives.

Nutrition:
- Info Per Servings 5g Carbs, 1g Protein, 13g Fat, 170 Calories

Coconut, Green Beans, And Shrimp Curry Soup

Servings: 4
Cooking Time: 20 Minutes
Ingredients:
- 2 tbsp ghee
- 1 lb jumbo shrimp, peeled and deveined
- 2 tsp ginger-garlic puree
- 2 tbsp red curry paste
- 6 oz coconut milk
- Salt and chili pepper to taste
- 1 bunch green beans, halved

Directions:
1. Melt ghee in a medium saucepan over medium heat. Add the shrimp, season with salt and pepper, and cook until they are opaque, 2 to 3 minutes. Remove shrimp to a plate. Add the ginger-garlic puree and red curry paste to the ghee and sauté for 2 minutes until fragrant.
2. Stir in the coconut milk; add the shrimp, salt, chili pepper, and green beans. Cook for 4 minutes. Reduce the heat to a simmer and cook an additional 3 minutes, occasionally stirring. Adjust taste with salt, fetch soup into serving bowls, and serve with cauli rice.

Nutrition:
- Info Per Servings 2g Carbs, 9g Protein, 35.4g Fat, 375 Calories

Arugula Prawn Salad With Mayo Dressing

Servings: 4
Cooking Time: 15 Minutes
Ingredients:
- 4 cups baby arugula
- ½ cup garlic mayonnaise
- 3 tbsp olive oil
- 1 lb tiger prawns, peeled and deveined
- 1 tsp Dijon mustard
- Salt and chili pepper to season
- 2 tbsp lemon juice

Directions:
1. Add the mayonnaise, lemon juice and mustard in a small bowl. Mix until smooth and creamy. Heat 2 tbps of olive oil in a skillet over medium heat, add the prawns, season with salt, and chili pepper, and fry in the oil for 3 minutes on each side until prawns are pink. Set aside to a plate.
2. Place the arugula in a serving bowl and pour half of the dressing on the salad. Toss with 2 spoons until mixed, and add the remaining dressing. Divide salad into 4 plates and serve with prawns.

Nutrition:
- Info Per Servings 2g Carbs, 8g Protein, 20.3g Fat, 215 Calories

Shrimp With Avocado & Cauliflower Salad

Servings: 6
Cooking Time: 30 Minutes
Ingredients:
- 1 cauliflower head, florets only
- 1 pound medium shrimp
- ¼ cup + 1 tbsp olive oil
- 1 avocado, chopped
- 3 tbsp chopped dill
- ¼ cup lemon juice
- 2 tbsp lemon zest
- Salt and black pepper to taste

Directions:
1. Heat 1 tbsp olive oil in a skillet and cook the shrimp until opaque, about 8-10 minutes. Place the cauliflower florets in a microwave-safe bowl, and microwave for 5 minutes. Place the shrimp, cauliflower, and avocado in a large bowl.
2. Whisk together the remaining olive oil, lemon zest, juice, dill, and some salt and pepper, in another bowl. Pour the dressing over, toss to combine and serve immediately.

Nutrition:
- Info Per Servings 5g Carbs, 15g Protein, 17g Fat, 214 Calories

Desserts And Drinks Recipes

Blackcurrant Iced Tea

Servings: 4
Cooking Time: 8 Minutes
Ingredients:
- 6 unflavored tea bags
- 2 cups water
- ½ cup sugar-free blackcurrant extract
- Swerve to taste
- Ice cubes for serving
- Lemon slices to garnish, cut on the side

Directions:
1. Pour the ice cubes in a pitcher and place it in the fridge.
2. Bring the water to boil in a saucepan over medium heat for 3 minutes and turn the heat off. Stir in the sugar to dissolve and steep the tea bags in the water for 2 minutes.
3. Remove the bags after and let the tea cool down. Stir in the blackcurrant extract until well incorporated, remove the pitcher from the fridge, and pour the mixture over the ice cubes.
4. Let sit for 3 minutes to cool and after, pour the mixture into tall glasses. Add some more ice cubes, place the lemon slices on the rim of the glasses, and serve the tea cold.

Nutrition:
- Info Per Servings 5g Carbs, 0g Protein, 0g Fat, 22 Calories

Brownie Fudge Keto Style

Servings: 10
Cooking Time: 6 Hours
Ingredients:
- ¾ cup coconut milk
- 1 teaspoon erythritol
- 2 tablespoons butter, melted
- 4 egg yolks, beaten
- 5 tablespoons cacao powder

Directions:
1. Mix all ingredients in a slow cooker and cook on low settings for 6 hours.
2. Serve and enjoy.

Nutrition:
- Info Per Servings 1.2g Carbs, 1.5g Protein, 8.4g Fat, 86 Calories

Blackberry Cheese Vanilla Blocks

Servings: 5
Cooking Time: 20mins
Ingredients:
- ½ cup blackberries
- 6 eggs
- 4 oz mascarpone cheese
- 1 tsp vanilla extract
- 4 tbsp stevia
- 8 oz melted coconut oil
- ½ tsp baking powder

Directions:
1. Except for blackberries, blend all ingredients in a blender until smooth.
2. Combine blackberries with blended mixture and transfer to a baking dish.
3. Bake blackberries mixture in the oven at 320°F for 20 minutes. Serve.

Nutrition:
- Info Per Servings 15g Carbs, 13g Protein, 4g Fat, 199 Calories

Mint Chocolate Protein Shake

Servings: 4
Cooking Time: 4 Minutes
Ingredients:
- 3 cups flax milk, chilled
- 3 tsp unsweetened cocoa powder
- 1 avocado, pitted, peeled, sliced
- 1 cup coconut milk, chilled
- 3 mint leaves + extra to garnish
- 3 tbsp erythritol
- 1 tbsp low carb Protein powder
- Whipping cream for topping

Directions:
1. Combine the milk, cocoa powder, avocado, coconut milk, mint leaves, erythritol, and protein powder into a blender, and blend for 1 minute until smooth.
2. Pour into serving glasses, lightly add some whipping cream on top, and garnish with mint leaves.

Nutrition:
- Info Per Servings 4g Carbs, 15g Protein, 14.5g Fat, 191 Calories

Hazelnut And Coconut Shake

Servings: 1
Cooking Time: 0 Minutes
Ingredients:
- ¼ coconut milk
- ¼ cup hazelnut, chopped
- 2 tbsps MCT oil or coconut oil
- 1 ½ cups water
- 1 packet Stevia, optional

Directions:
1. Add all ingredients in a blender.
2. Blend until smooth and creamy.
3. Serve and enjoy.

Nutrition:
- Info Per Servings 8.9g Carbs, 6.5g Protein, 62.1g Fat, 591 Calories

Spicy Cheese Crackers

Servings: 4
Cooking Time: 10 Mins
Ingredients:
- 3/4 cup almond flour
- 1 egg
- 2 tablespoons cream cheese
- 2 cups shredded Parmesan cheese
- 1/2 teaspoon red pepper flakes
- 1 tablespoon dry ranch salad dressing mix

Directions:
1. Preheat oven to 425 degrees F.
2. Combine Parmesan and cream cheese in a microwave safe bowl and microwave in 30 second intervals. Add the cheese to mix well, and whisk along the almond flour, egg, ranch seasoning, and red pepper flakes, stirring occasionally.
3. Transfer the dough in between two parchment-lined baking sheets. Form the dough into rolls by cutting off plum-sized pieces of dough with dough cutter into 1-inch square pieces, yielding about 60 pieces.
4. Place crackers to a baking sheet lined parchment. Bake for 5 minutes, flipping halfway, then continue to bake for 5 minutes more. Chill before serving.

Nutrition:
- Info Per Servings 18g Carbs, 17g Protein, 4g Fat, 235 Calories

Coconut Fat Bombs

Servings: 4
Cooking Time: 22 Minutes +cooling Time
Ingredients:
- 2/3 cup coconut oil, melted
- 1 can coconut milk
- 18 drops stevia liquid
- 1 cup unsweetened coconut flakes

Directions:
1. Mix the coconut oil with the milk and stevia to combine. Stir in the coconut flakes until well distributed. Pour into silicone muffin molds and freeze for 1 hour to harden.

Nutrition:
- Info Per Servings 2g Carbs, 4g Protein, 19g Fat, 214 Calories

Coco-loco Creamy Shake

Servings: 1
Cooking Time: 0 Minutes
Ingredients:
- ½ cup coconut milk
- 2 tbsp Dutch-processed cocoa powder, unsweetened
- 1 cup brewed coffee, chilled
- 1 tbsp hemp seeds
- 1-2 packets Stevia
- 3 tbsps MCT oil or coconut oil

Directions:
1. Add all ingredients in a blender.
2. Blend until smooth and creamy.
3. Serve and enjoy.

Nutrition:
- Info Per Servings 10.2g Carbs, 5.4g Protein, 61.1g Fat, 567 Calories

Granny Smith Apple Tart

Servings: 8
Cooking Time: 65 Minutes
Ingredients:
- 6 tbsp butter
- 2 cups almond flour
- 1 tsp cinnamon
- ⅓ cup sweetener
- Filling:
- 2 cups sliced Granny Smith
- ¼ cup butter
- ¼ cup sweetener
- ½ tsp cinnamon
- ½ tsp lemon juice
- Topping:
- ¼ tsp cinnamon
- 2 tbsp sweetener

Directions:
1. Preheat your oven to 370°F and combine all crust ingredients in a bowl. Press this mixture into the bottom of a greased pan. Bake for 5 minutes.
2. Meanwhile, combine the apples and lemon juice in a bowl and let them sit until the crust is ready. Arrange them on top of the crust. Combine the rest of the filling ingredients, and brush this mixture over the apples. Bake for about 30 minutes.
3. Press the apples down with a spatula, return to oven, and bake for 20 more minutes. Combine the cinnamon and sweetener, in a bowl, and sprinkle over the tart.
4. Note: Granny Smith apples have just 9.5g of net carbs per 100g. Still high for you? Substitute with Chayote squash, which has the same texture and rich nutrients, and just around 4g of net carbs.

Nutrition:
- Info Per Servings 6.7g Carbs, 7g Protein, 26g Fat, 302 Calories

Blueberry Tart With Lavender

Servings: 6
Cooking Time: 2 Hours 25 Minutes
Ingredients:
- 1 large low carb pie crust
- 1 ½ cups heavy cream
- 2 tbsp swerve
- 1 tbsp culinary lavender
- 1 vanilla, seeds extracted
- 2 cups fresh blueberries
- Erythritol for topping

Directions:
1. Preheat the oven to 400°F. Place the pie crust with its pan on a baking tray and bake in the oven for 30 minutes, until golden brown; remove and let cool.
2. Mix the heavy cream and lavender in a saucepan. Set the pan over medium heat and bring the mixture to a boil; turn the heat off and let cool. Refrigerate for 1 hour to infuse the cream.
3. Remove the cream from the fridge and strain through a colander into a bowl to remove the lavender pieces. Mix swerve and vanilla into the cream, and pour into the cooled crust. Scatter the blueberries on and refrigerate the pie for 45 minutes. Remove and top with erythritol, before slicing.

Nutrition:
- Info Per Servings 10.7g Carbs, 3.3g Protein, 16.4g Fat, 198 Calories

Chocolate Cakes

Servings: 6
Cooking Time: 25 Minutes
Ingredients:
- ½ cup almond flour
- ¼ cup xylitol
- 1 tsp baking powder
- ½ tsp baking soda
- 1 tsp cinnamon, ground
- A pinch of salt
- A pinch of ground cloves
- ½ cup butter, melted
- ½ cup buttermilk
- 1 egg
- 1 tsp pure almond extract
- For the Frosting:
- 1 cup double cream
- 1 cup dark chocolate, flaked

Directions:
1. Preheat the oven to 360°F. Use a cooking spray to grease a donut pan.
2. In a bowl, mix the cloves, almond flour, baking powder, salt, baking soda, xylitol, and cinnamon. In a separate bowl, combine the almond extract, butter, egg, buttermilk, and cream. Mix the wet mixture into the dry mixture. Evenly ladle the batter into the donut pan. Bake for 17 minutes.
3. Set a pan over medium heat and warm double cream; simmer for 2 minutes. Fold in the chocolate flakes; combine until all the chocolate melts; let cool. Spread the top of the cakes with the frosting.

Nutrition:
- Info Per Servings 10g Carbs, 4.8g Protein, 20g Fat, 218 Calories

Choco Coffee Milk Shake

Servings: 1
Cooking Time: 0 Minutes
Ingredients:
- ½ cup coconut milk
- 1 tbsp cocoa powder
- 1 cup brewed coffee, chilled
- 1 packet Stevia, or more to taste
- ½ tsp cinnamon
- 5 tbsps coconut oil

Directions:
1. Add all ingredients in a blender.
2. Blend until smooth and creamy.
3. Serve and enjoy.

Nutrition:
- Info Per Servings 10g Carbs, 4.1g Protein, 97.4g Fat, 880 Calories

Vanilla Ice Cream

Servings: 4
Cooking Time: 50 Minutes + Cooling Time
Ingredients:
- ½ cup smooth peanut butter
- ½ cup swerve
- 3 cups half and half
- 1 tsp vanilla extract
- 2 pinches salt

Directions:
1. Beat peanut butter and swerve in a bowl with a hand mixer until smooth. Gradually whisk in half and half until thoroughly combined. Mix in vanilla and salt. Pour mixture into a loaf pan and freeze for 45 minutes until firmed up. Scoop into glasses when ready to eat and serve.

Nutrition:
- Info Per Servings 6g Carbs, 13g Protein, 23g Fat, 290 Calories

Coconut Macadamia Nut Bombs

Servings: 4
Cooking Time: 0 Mins
Ingredients:
- 2 packets stevia
- 5 tbsps unsweetened coconut powder
- 10 tbsps coconut oil
- 3 tbsps chopped macadamia nuts
- Salt to taste

Directions:
1. Heat the coconut oil in a pan over medium heat. Add coconut powder, stevia and salt, stirring to combined well; then remove from heat.
2. Spoon mixture into a lined mini muffin pan. Place in the freezer for a few hours.
3. Sprinkle nuts over the mixture before serving.

Nutrition:
- Info Per Servings 0.2g Carbs, 1.1g Protein, 15.2g Fat, 143 Calories

Coconut Raspberry Bars

Servings: 12
Cooking Time: 20 Minutes
Ingredients:
- 1 cup coconut milk
- 3 cups desiccated coconut
- 1/3 cup erythritol powder
- 1 cup raspberries, pulsed
- ½ cup coconut oil or other oils

Directions:
1. Preheat oven to 380oF.
2. Combine all ingredients in a mixing bowl.
3. Pour into a greased baking dish.
4. Bake in the oven for 20 minutes.
5. Let it rest for 10 minutes.
6. Serve and enjoy.

Nutrition:
- Info Per Servings 8.2g Carbs, 1.5g Protein, 14.7g Fat, 170 Calories

Creamy Coconut Kiwi Drink

Servings: 4
Cooking Time: 3 Minutes
Ingredients:
- 6 kiwis, pulp scooped
- 3 tbsp erythritol or to taste
- 3 cups unsweetened coconut milk
- 2 cups coconut cream
- 7 ice cubes
- Mint leaves to garnish

Directions:
1. In a blender, process the kiwis, erythritol, milk, cream, and ice cubes until smooth, about 3 minutes. Pour into four serving glasses, garnish with mint leaves, and serve.

Nutrition:
- Info Per Servings 1g Carbs, 16g Protein, 38g Fat, 425 Calories

Blueberry Ice Pops

Servings: 6
Cooking Time: 5 Minutes + Cooling Time
Ingredients:
- 3 cups blueberries
- ½ tbsp lemon juice
- ¼ cup swerve
- ¼ cup water

Directions:
1. Pour the blueberries, lemon juice, swerve, and water in a blender, and puree on high speed for 2 minutes until smooth. Strain through a sieve into a bowl, discard the solids.
2. Mix in more water if too thick. Divide the mixture into ice pop molds, insert stick cover, and freeze for 4 hours to 1 week. When ready to serve, dip in warm water and remove the pops.

Nutrition:
- Info Per Servings 7.9g Carbs, 2.3g Protein, 1.2g Fat, 48 Calories

Berry-choco Goodness Shake

Servings: 1
Cooking Time: 0 Minutes
Ingredients:
- ½ cup half and half
- ¼ cup raspberries
- ¼ cup blackberry
- ¼ cup strawberries, chopped
- 3 tbsps avocado oil
- 1 packet Stevia, or more to taste
- 1 tbsp cocoa powder
- 1 ½ cups water

Directions:
1. Add all ingredients in a blender.
2. Blend until smooth and creamy.
3. Serve and enjoy.

Nutrition:
- Info Per Servings 7g Carbs, 4.4g Protein, 43.3g Fat, 450 Calories

Crispy Zucchini Chips

Servings: 5
Cooking Time: 20 Mins
Ingredients:
- 1 large egg, beaten
- 1 cup. almond flour
- 1 medium zucchini, thinly sliced
- 3/4 cup Parmesan cheese, grated
- Cooking spray

Directions:
1. Preheat oven to 400 degrees F. Line a baking pan with parchment paper.
2. In a bowl, mix together Parmesan cheese and almond flour.
3. In another bowl whisk the egg. Dip each zucchini slice in the egg, then the cheese mixture until finely coated.
4. Spray zucchini slices with cooking spray and place in the prepared oven.
5. Bake for 20 minutes until crispy. Serve.

Nutrition:
- Info Per Servings 16.8g Carbs, 10.8g Protein, 6g Fat, 215.2 Calories

Green And Fruity Smoothie

Servings: 2
Cooking Time: 0 Minutes
Ingredients:
- 1 cup spinach, packed
- ½ cup strawberries, chopped
- ½ avocado, peeled, pitted, and frozen
- 1 tbsp almond butter
- ¼ cup packed kale, stem discarded, and leaves chopped
- 1 cup ice-cold water
- 5 tablespoons MCT oil or coconut oil

Directions:
1. Blend all ingredients in a blender until smooth and creamy.
2. Serve and enjoy.

Nutrition:
- Info Per Servings 10g Carbs, 1.6g Protein, 47.3g Fat, 459 Calories

Baby Kale And Yogurt Smoothie

Servings: 1
Cooking Time: 0 Minutes
Ingredients:
- ½ cup whole milk yogurt
- ½ cup baby kale greens
- 1 packet Stevia, or more to taste
- 3 tbsps MCT oil
- ½ tbsp sunflower seeds
- 1 cup water

Directions:
1. Add all ingredients in a blender.
2. Blend until smooth and creamy.
3. Serve and enjoy.

Nutrition:
- Info Per Servings 2.6g Carbs, 11.0g Protein, 26.2g Fat, 329 Calories

Choco-chia Pudding

Servings: 4
Cooking Time: 5 Minutes
Ingredients:
- ¼ cup fresh or frozen raspberries
- 1 scoop chocolate protein powder
- 1 cup unsweetened almond milk
- 3 tbsp Chia seeds
- 1 tsp Stevia (optional)
- 5 tablespoons coconut oil

Directions:
1. Mix the chocolate protein powder and almond milk.
2. Add the chia seeds and mix well with a whisk or a fork. Add the coconut oil.
3. Flavor with Stevia depending on the desired sweetness.
4. Let it rest for 5 minutes and continue stirring.
5. Serve and enjoy.

Nutrition:
- Info Per Servings 10g Carbs, 11.5g Protein, 19.6g Fat, 243.5 Calories

Almond Butter Fat Bombs

Servings: 4
Cooking Time: 3 Minutes + Cooling Time
Ingredients:
- ½ cup almond butter
- ½ cup coconut oil
- 4 tbsp unsweetened cocoa powder
- ½ cup erythritol

Directions:
1. Melt butter and coconut oil in the microwave for 45 seconds, stirring twice until properly melted and mixed. Mix in cocoa powder and erythritol until completely combined.
2. Pour into muffin moulds and refrigerate for 3 hours to harden.

Nutrition:
- Info Per Servings 2g Carbs, 4g Protein, 18.3g Fat, 193 Calories

Raspberry Nut Truffles

Servings: 4
Cooking Time: 6 Minutes + Cooling Time
Ingredients:
- 2 cups raw cashews
- 2 tbsp flax seed
- 1 ½ cups sugar-free raspberry preserves
- 3 tbsp swerve
- 10 oz unsweetened chocolate chips
- 3 tbsp olive oil

Directions:
1. Line a baking sheet with parchment paper and set aside. Grind the cashews and flax seeds in a blender for 45 seconds until smoothly crushed; add the raspberry and 2 tbsp of swerve.
2. Process further for 1 minute until well combined. Form 1-inch balls of the mixture, place on the baking sheet, and freeze for 1 hour or until firmed up.
3. Melt the chocolate chips, oil, and 1tbsp of swerve in a microwave for 1 ½ minutes. Toss the truffles to coat in the chocolate mixture, put on the baking sheet, and freeze further for at least 2 hours.

Nutrition:
- Info Per Servings 3.5g Carbs, 12g Protein, 18.3g Fat, 251 Calories

Raspberry-choco Shake

Servings: 1
Cooking Time: 0 Minutes
Ingredients:
- ¼ cup heavy cream, liquid
- 1 tbsp cocoa powder
- 1 packet Stevia, or more to taste
- ¼ cup raspberries
- 1 ½ cups water

Directions:
1. Add all ingredients in a blender.
2. Blend until smooth and creamy.
3. Serve and enjoy.

Nutrition:
- Info Per Servings 11.1g Carbs, 3.8g Protein, 45.0g Fat, 438 Calories

Almond Choco Shake

Servings: 1
Cooking Time: 0 Minutes
Ingredients:
- ½ cup heavy cream, liquid
- 1 tbsp cocoa powder
- 1 packet Stevia, or more to taste
- 5 almonds, chopped
- 1 ½ cups water
- 3 tbsp coconut oil

Directions:
1. Add all ingredients in a blender.
2. Blend until smooth and creamy.
3. Serve and enjoy.

Nutrition:
- Info Per Servings 9.7g Carbs, 11.9g Protein, 45.9g Fat, 485 Calories

Coffee Fat Bombs

Servings: 6
Cooking Time: 3 Minutes + Cooling Time
Ingredients:
- 1 ½ cups mascarpone cheese
- ½ cup melted butter
- 3 tbsp unsweetened cocoa powder
- ¼ cup erythritol
- 6 tbsp brewed coffee, room temperature

Directions:
1. Whisk the mascarpone cheese, butter, cocoa powder, erythritol, and coffee with a hand mixer until creamy and fluffy, for 1 minute. Fill into muffin tins and freeze for 3 hours until firm.

Nutrition:
- Info Per Servings 2g Carbs, 4g Protein, 14g Fat, 145 Calories

Raspberry Sorbet

Servings: 1
Cooking Time: 3 Minutes
Ingredients:
- ¼ tsp vanilla extract
- 1 packet gelatine, without sugar
- 1 tbsp heavy whipping cream
- ⅓ cup boiling water
- 2 tbsp mashed raspberries
- 1 ½ cups crushed Ice
- ⅓ cup cold water

Directions:
1. Combine the gelatin and boiling water, until completely dissolved; then transfer to a blender. Add the remaining ingredients. Blend until smooth and freeze for at least 2 hours.

Nutrition:
- Info Per Servings 3.7g Carbs, 4g Protein, 10g Fat, 173 Calories

49 day meal plan

Day 1

Breakfast: Herb Butter With Parsley 22

Lunch: Chicken, Broccoli & Cashew Stir-fry 46

Dinner: Grilled Steak Salad With Pickled Peppers 78

Day 2

Breakfast: Portobello Mushroom Burgers 22

Lunch: Chipotle Salmon Asparagus 37

Dinner: Beef Reuben Soup 78

Day 3

Breakfast: Mushroom & Cauliflower Bake 23

Lunch: Bacon & Cheese Chicken 46

Dinner: Chicken Creamy Soup 79

Day 4

Breakfast: Cauliflower Gouda Casserole 23

Lunch: Chicken Goujons With Tomato Sauce 47

Dinner: Caesar Salad With Smoked Salmon And Poached Eggs 79

Day 5

Breakfast: Roasted Brussels Sprouts With Sunflower Seeds 24

Lunch: Lemon Threaded Chicken Skewers 47

Dinner: Balsamic Cucumber Salad 80

Day 6

Breakfast: Morning Granola 24

Lunch: Chili Lime Chicken 48

Dinner: Slow Cooker Beer Soup With Cheddar & Sausage 80

Day 7

Breakfast: Zucchini Noodles 25

Lunch: Parmesan Wings With Yogurt Sauce 48

Dinner: Cream Of Thyme Tomato Soup 81

Day 8

Breakfast: Asparagus And Tarragon Flan 25

Lunch: Chili Turkey Patties With Cucumber Salsa 49

Dinner: Spicy Chicken Bean Soup 81

Day 9

Breakfast: Vegetarian Burgers 26

Lunch: Stir Fried Broccoli 'n Chicken 49

Dinner: Citrusy Brussels Sprouts Salad 82

Day 10

Breakfast: Spicy Tofu With Worcestershire Sauce 26

Lunch: Chicken Country Style 50

Dinner: Simplified French Onion Soup 82

Day 11

Breakfast: Tofu Stir Fry With Asparagus 27

Lunch: Baked Chicken Pesto 51

Dinner: Green Minestrone Soup 83

Day 12

Breakfast: Cauliflower Fritters 27

Lunch: Greek Chicken With Capers 51

Dinner: Creamy Cauliflower Soup With Bacon Chips 83

Day 13

Breakfast: Grated Cauliflower With Seasoned Mayo 28

Lunch: Chicken Stew With Sun-dried Tomatoes 52

Dinner: Butternut And Kale Soup 84

Day 14

Breakfast: Vegan Mushroom Pizza 28

Lunch: Turkey & Cheese Stuffed Mushrooms 53

Dinner: Warm Baby Artichoke Salad 84

Day 15

Breakfast: Cilantro-lime Guacamole 29

Lunch: Chicken With Asparagus & Root Vegetables 54

Dinner: Coconut, Green Beans, And Shrimp Curry Soup 85

Day 16

Breakfast: Easy Cauliflower Soup 29

Lunch: Turkey Stew With Salsa Verde 55

Dinner: Arugula Prawn Salad With Mayo Dressing 85

Day 17

Breakfast: Stuffed Portobello Mushrooms 30

Lunch: Chicken In Creamy Mushroom Sauce 56

Dinner: Shrimp With Avocado & Cauliflower Salad 86

Day 18

Breakfast: Tomato Stuffed Avocado 30

Lunch: Chicken Breasts With Cheddar & Pepperoni 57

Dinner: Shrimp In Curry Sauce 39

Day 19

Breakfast: Strawberry Mug Cake 30

Lunch: Chicken In Creamy Tomato Sauce 58

Dinner: Simply Steamed Alaskan Cod 40

Day 20

Breakfast: Creamy Cucumber Avocado Soup 31

Lunch: Chicken With Anchovy Tapenade 59

Dinner: Golden Pompano In Microwave 40

Day 21

Breakfast: Greek Styled Veggie-rice 31

Lunch: Yummy Chicken Queso 60

Dinner: Steamed Asparagus And Shrimps 41

Day 22

Breakfast: Greek-style Zucchini Pasta 32

Lunch: Garlic Beef & Egg Frittata 62

Dinner: Avocado Salad With Shrimp 41

Day 23

Breakfast: Classic Tangy Ratatouille 32

Lunch: Chicken Broth Beef Roast 63

Dinner: Avocado And Salmon 42

Day 24

Breakfast: Pumpkin Bake 33

Lunch: Beef Cauliflower Curry 63

Dinner: Grilled Shrimp With Chimichurri Sauce 42

Day 25

Breakfast: Coconut Cauliflower Rice 33

Lunch: Mushroom Beef Stew 64

Dinner: Steamed Mustard Salmon 43

Day 26

Breakfast: Devilled Eggs With Sriracha Mayo 11

Lunch: Beef And Feta Salad 64

Dinner: Lemon Marinated Salmon With Spices 43

Day 27

Breakfast: Cheddar Cheese Chips 12

Lunch: Beef Skewers With Ranch Dressing 65

Dinner: Chili-lime Shrimps 44

Day 28

Breakfast: Cheesy Lettuce Rolls 12

Lunch: Beef Zucchini Boats 65

Dinner: Air Fryer Seasoned Salmon Fillets 44

Day 29

Breakfast: Sautéed Brussels Sprouts 12

Lunch: Homemade Classic Beef Burgers 66

Dinner: Bang Bang Shrimps 45

Day 30

Breakfast: Sour Cream And Carrot Sticks 13

Lunch: Garlicky Beef Stew 66

Dinner: Blackened Fish Tacos With Slaw 45

Day 31

Breakfast: Mascarpone Snapped Amaretti Biscuits 13

Lunch: Creamy Pork Chops 67

Dinner: Fat-burning Dressing 34

Day 32

Breakfast: Coconut Ginger Macaroons 14

Lunch: Classic Meatloaf 68

Dinner: Tzatziki 34

Day 33

Breakfast: Cranberry Sauce Meatballs 14

Lunch: Pancetta Sausage With Kale 69

Dinner: Caesar Dressing 35

Day 34

Breakfast: Bacon-wrapped Jalapeño Peppers 15

Lunch: Cocoa-crusted Pork Tenderloin 70

Dinner: Chunky Blue Cheese Dressing 35

Day 35

Breakfast: Baba Ganoush Eggplant Dip 15

Lunch: Beef Sausage Casserole 71

Dinner: Avocado Mayo 35

Day 36

Breakfast: Pesto Stuffed Mushrooms 16

Lunch: Italian Shredded Beef 71

Dinner: Vegetarian Fish Sauce 36

Day 37

Breakfast: Chocolate Mousse 16

Lunch: Spicy Mesquite Ribs 72

Dinner: Celery-onion Vinaigrette 36

Day 38

Breakfast: Cheesy Green Bean Crisps 17

Lunch: Beef Meatballs With Onion Sauce 73

Dinner: Brownie Fudge Keto Style 87

Day 39

Breakfast: Onion Cheese Muffins 17

Lunch: Rack Of Lamb In Red Bell Pepper Butter Sauce 74

Dinner: Blackberry Cheese Vanilla Blocks 87

Day 40

Breakfast: Keto "cornbread" 18

Lunch: Beef Steak Filipino Style 74

Dinner: Mint Chocolate Protein Shake 87

Day 41

Breakfast: Pecorino-mushroom Balls 18

Lunch: Russian Beef Gratin 75

Dinner: Hazelnut And Coconut Shake 88

Day 42

Breakfast: Simple Tender Crisp Cauli-bites 19

Lunch: Beef Mushroom Meatloaf 75

Dinner: Coconut Fat Bombs 88

Day 43

Breakfast: Choco And Coconut Bars 19

Lunch: Beef Cheeseburger Casserole 76

Dinner: Blueberry Ice Pops 92

Day 44

Breakfast: Mozzarella & Prosciutto Wraps 19

Lunch: One Pot Tomato Pork Chops Stew 76

Dinner: Green And Fruity Smoothie 93

Day 45

Breakfast: Keto Caprese Salad 20

Lunch: Moroccan Beef Stew 77

Dinner: Baby Kale And Yogurt Smoothie 94

Day 46

Breakfast: Cocktail Kielbasa With Mustard Sauce 20

Lunch: Meatballs With Ranch-buffalo Sauce 77

Dinner: Choco-chia Pudding 94

Day 47

Breakfast: Sweet And Hot Nuts 20

Lunch: Steamed Herbed Red Snapper 37

Dinner: Raspberry Nut Truffles 95

Day 48

Breakfast: Asian Glazed Meatballs 21

Lunch: Coconut Crab Patties 38

Dinner: Raspberry-choco Shake 95

Day 49

Breakfast: Balsamic Zucchini 21

Lunch: Lemon Chili Halibut 39

Dinner: Almond Choco Shake 95

RECIPES INDEX

A
Air Fryer Seasoned Salmon Fillets 44
Almond Butter Fat Bombs 94
Almond Choco Shake 95
Arugula Prawn Salad With Mayo Dressing 85
Asian Glazed Meatballs 21
Asparagus And Tarragon Flan 25
Avocado And Salmon 42
Avocado Mayo 35
Avocado Salad With Shrimp 41

B
Baba Ganoush Eggplant Dip 15
Baby Kale And Yogurt Smoothie 94
Bacon & Cheese Chicken 46
Bacon-wrapped Jalapeño Peppers 15
Baked Chicken Pesto 51
Baked Chicken With Acorn Squash And Goat's Cheese 54
Baked Cod And Tomato Capers Mix 38
Balsamic Cucumber Salad 80
Balsamic Zucchini 21
Bang Bang Shrimps 45
Basil Keto Crackers 11
Beef And Feta Salad 64
Beef Cauliflower Curry 63
Beef Cheeseburger Casserole 76
Beef Meatballs With Onion Sauce 73
Beef Mushroom Meatloaf 75
Beef Reuben Soup 78
Beef Sausage Casserole 71
Beef Skewers With Ranch Dressing 65
Beef Steak Filipino Style 74
Beef Stew With Bacon 67
Beef Zucchini Boats 65
Berry-choco Goodness Shake 93

Blackberry Cheese Vanilla Blocks 87
Blackcurrant Iced Tea 86
Blackened Fish Tacos With Slaw 45
Blueberry Ice Pops 92
Blueberry Tart With Lavender 90
Brownie Fudge Keto Style 87
Butternut And Kale Soup 84

C
Caesar Dressing 35
Caesar Salad With Smoked Salmon And Poached Eggs 79
Cajun Spiced Pecans(2) 16
Cauliflower Fritters 27
Cauliflower Gouda Casserole 23
Celery-onion Vinaigrette 36
Cheddar Cheese Chips 12
Cheesy Green Bean Crisps 17
Cheesy Lettuce Rolls 12
Chicken Breasts With Cheddar & Pepperoni 57
Chicken Broth Beef Roast 63
Chicken Country Style 50
Chicken Creamy Soup 79
Chicken Goujons With Tomato Sauce 47
Chicken In Creamy Mushroom Sauce 56
Chicken In Creamy Tomato Sauce 58
Chicken Paella With Chorizo 60
Chicken Stew With Sun-dried Tomatoes 52
Chicken With Anchovy Tapenade 59
Chicken With Asparagus & Root Vegetables 54
Chicken, Broccoli & Cashew Stir-fry 46
Chili Lime Chicken 48
Chili Turkey Patties With Cucumber Salsa 49
Chili-lime Shrimps 44
Chipotle Salmon Asparagus 37
Choco And Coconut Bars 19
Choco Coffee Milk Shake 91

Choco-chia Pudding 94
Chocolate Cakes 90
Chocolate Mousse 16
Chunky Blue Cheese Dressing 35
Cilantro-lime Guacamole 29
Citrusy Brussels Sprouts Salad 82
Classic Meatloaf 68
Classic Tangy Ratatouille 32
Cocktail Kielbasa With Mustard Sauce 20
Cocoa-crusted Pork Tenderloin 70
Coco-loco Creamy Shake 89
Coconut Cauliflower Rice 33
Coconut Crab Patties 38
Coconut Fat Bombs 88
Coconut Ginger Macaroons 14
Coconut Macadamia Nut Bombs 91
Coconut Raspberry Bars 92
Coconut, Green Beans, And Shrimp Curry Soup 85
Coffee Fat Bombs 96
Cranberry Sauce Meatballs 14
Cream Of Thyme Tomato Soup 81
Creamy Cauliflower Soup With Bacon Chips 83
Creamy Coconut Kiwi Drink 92
Creamy Cucumber Avocado Soup 31
Creamy Pork Chops 67
Creamy Stuffed Chicken With Parma Ham 61
Crispy Zucchini Chips 93

D
Devilled Eggs With Sriracha Mayo 11

E
Easy Cauliflower Soup 29
Eggplant & Tomato Braised Chicken Thighs 59

F
Fat-burning Dressing 34

G
Garlic Beef & Egg Frittata 62
Garlicky Beef Stew 66

Golden Pompano In Microwave 40
Granny Smith Apple Tart 89
Grated Cauliflower With Seasoned Mayo 28
Greek Chicken With Capers 51
Greek Styled Veggie-rice 31
Greek-style Zucchini Pasta 32
Green And Fruity Smoothie 93
Green Minestrone Soup 83
Grilled Flank Steak With Lime Vinaigrette 72
Grilled Shrimp With Chimichurri Sauce 42
Grilled Steak Salad With Pickled Peppers 78

H
Habanero Chicken Wings 53
Hazelnut And Coconut Shake 88
Herb Butter With Parsley 22
Homemade Classic Beef Burgers 66

I
Italian Shredded Beef 71

K
Keto "cornbread" 18
Keto Caprese Salad 20

L
Lemon & Rosemary Chicken In A Skillet 56
Lemon Chicken Bake 62
Lemon Chili Halibut 39
Lemon Marinated Salmon With Spices 43
Lemon Threaded Chicken Skewers 47

M
Mascarpone Snapped Amaretti Biscuits 13
Meatballs With Ranch-buffalo Sauce 77
Mint Chocolate Protein Shake 87
Morning Granola 24
Moroccan Beef Stew 77
Mozzarella & Prosciutto Wraps 19
Mushroom & Cauliflower Bake 23
Mushroom Beef Stew 64

N

North African Lamb 70

O

One Pot Tomato Pork Chops Stew 76

One-pot Chicken With Mushrooms And Spinach 61

Onion Cheese Muffins 17

P

Pancetta Sausage With Kale 69

Parmesan Wings With Yogurt Sauce 48

Pecorino-mushroom Balls 18

Pesto Stuffed Mushrooms 16

Pork Osso Bucco 68

Portobello Mushroom Burgers 22

Pumpkin Bake 33

R

Rack Of Lamb In Red Bell Pepper Butter Sauce 74

Raspberry Nut Truffles 95

Raspberry Sorbet 96

Raspberry-choco Shake 95

Roasted Brussels Sprouts With Sunflower Seeds 24

Russian Beef Gratin 75

S

Sautéed Brussels Sprouts 12

Shrimp In Curry Sauce 39

Shrimp With Avocado & Cauliflower Salad 86

Simple Tender Crisp Cauli-bites 19

Simplified French Onion Soup 82

Simply Steamed Alaskan Cod 40

Slow Cooker Beer Soup With Cheddar & Sausage 80

Slow-cooked Mexican Turkey Soup 55

Sour Cream And Carrot Sticks 13

Spanish Frittata 73

Spicy Cheese Crackers 88

Spicy Chicken Bean Soup 81

Spicy Mesquite Ribs 72

Spicy Sea Bass With Hazelnuts 38

Spicy Tofu With Worcestershire Sauce 26

Spinach & Ricotta Stuffed Chicken Breasts 58

Steamed Asparagus And Shrimps 41

Steamed Herbed Red Snapper 37

Steamed Mustard Salmon 43

Stir Fried Broccoli 'n Chicken 49

Strawberry Mug Cake 30

Stuffed Portobello Mushrooms 30

Sweet And Hot Nuts 20

Sweet Chipotle Grilled Ribs 69

T

Thyme Chicken Thighs 52

Tofu Stir Fry With Asparagus 27

Tomato Stuffed Avocado 30

Turkey & Cheese Stuffed Mushrooms 53

Turkey Breast Salad 50

Turkey Stew With Salsa Verde 55

Tzatziki 34

V

Vanilla Ice Cream 91

Vegan Mushroom Pizza 28

Vegetarian Burgers 26

Vegetarian Fish Sauce 36

W

Warm Baby Artichoke Salad 84

Y

Yummy Chicken Queso 60

Z

Zesty Grilled Chicken 57

Zucchini Noodles 25